Teacher's Guide to
Bet Is for B'reishit
Hebrew for Adults
Book 3

Tav Is for Torah
Hebrew for Adults
Book 4

Linda Motzkin
The author of
Aleph Isn't Tough and
Aleph Isn't Enough

Hara Person, series editor

Table of Contents

Introduction

Bet Is for B'reishit and *Tav Is for Torah* are the final two books in the URJ's program of Hebrew learning for adults. They are presented together in this Teacher's Guide because the two books share the same format. Like the books that preceded them in this series, *Bet Is for B'reishit* and *Tav Is for Torah* are designed for English-speaking adults who primarily encounter the Hebrew language through their participation in Jewish religious life. Unlike the second book in the series, *Aleph Isn't Enough*, which was structured around selected prayer book excerpts, these third and fourth books are organized around passages from the Torah. The material presented in these books is cumulative: *Bet Is for B'reishit* assumes knowledge of the vocabulary, roots, and grammatical material presented in *Aleph Isn't Enough*, and *Tav Is for Torah* assumes the same regarding *Bet Is for B'reishit*.

Goals

As in *Aleph Isn't Enough*, the goal of *Bet Is for B'reishit* and *Tav Is for Torah* is to provide students with a greater understanding and appreciation of the Hebrew that they encounter in contemporary Jewish religious life. Building upon the foundation established in *Aleph Isn't Enough*, *Bet Is for B'reishit* and *Tav Is for Torah* further the development of comprehension and translation skills, introducing new Hebrew roots, vocabulary words, and basic grammatical structures, and providing students with reading and translation practice drawn from the Bible, prayer book, and Jewish life. Exercises at the end of each chapter reinforce the Hebrew material introduced in the chapter.

Bet Is for B'reishit and *Tav Is for Torah* have an additional goal: to provide students with an introduction to the time-honored Jewish practice of Torah study. Each unit of study is organized around a selected passage from the Torah, including several different translations as well as an array of commentaries drawn from classical and contemporary sources. The commentaries all take as their point of departure some Hebrew detail within the Torah study passage. The Torah study passage also illustrates the grammatical concepts introduced in each unit and contains the new Hebrew roots and vocabulary words for that unit.

As in *Aleph Isn't Enough*, the overall goal of enriching our students' understanding and appreciation of Hebrew is supported in *Bet Is for B'reishit* and *Tav Is for Torah* with a wealth of supplemental material. This material includes examples of ancient and modern usages of Hebrew roots, grammar enrichment charts and explanations, sections that present extra information on Jewish practices and concepts, and selections from classical and contemporary Hebrew literature. Incorporating some or all of this material into the classroom can enhance and enrich the students' learning experience.

Methodology

Bet Is for B'reishit and *Tav Is for Torah* are divided into five units of two chapters each, for a total of ten chapters in each book. This format provides the student with an opportunity to delve into a Torah passage, while the learning of new vocabulary, Hebrew roots, and grammatical material is spread over two sessions. The first chapter in each unit presents the Torah Study Text for that unit, along with translations, commentary, vocabulary, and Hebrew roots. The second chapter in each unit provides a review of the previous chapter's vocabulary and roots within the Torah Study Text and introduces the new Building Blocks (grammatical concepts) for that unit, along with grammar enrichment. Both chapters contain exercises and various types of supplemental material. Since the two chapters function as a single unit, the sequence in which the material can be introduced is flexible. Some teachers may prefer to introduce some of the material in the second chapter before completing the first chapter.

The first chapter of each unit includes the following sections.

Torah Study Text

Each unit begins with a Torah Study Text, five to nine verses long. The passages in *Bet Is for B'reishit* all come from Genesis, while *Tav Is for Torah* includes passages from four of the five books of the Torah. The Torah Study Texts are all well-known passages (e.g., the first day of Creation, the Tower of Babel, Jacob's ladder, Moses at the Burning Bush, the Ten Commandments), and they contain the vocabulary words and Hebrew roots to be introduced in that unit. They also illustrate the new grammatical concepts (Building Blocks) for that unit.

Unlike the prayer book excerpts that began each chapter in *Aleph Isn't Enough*, the Hebrew of these Torah Study Texts is unlikely to be familiar to students, even though students may be familiar with these passages in English translation. For that reason, the opening activity is not designed as a Hebrew Reading Practice, but as Torah Text Study. It is not necessary for students to work on achieving fluency in reading these Hebrew passages aloud, as they are generally not read aloud as a community in Jewish prayer services or ritual. It is more useful for students to begin each unit by examining the unfamiliar Hebrew of these Torah Study Texts to pick out the elements that they have learned and can recognize. (Words, roots, prefixes, and suffixes that have already been introduced are indicated in this Teacher's Guide.) As the students progress, more and more of the Hebrew will become familiar to them.

Translating the Torah Study Text

The chapter then provides a word-by-word translation of the Torah Study Text. This enables students to recognize in context words or grammatical structures that they may have previously learned but been unable to identify within the unfamiliar Hebrew text. It also gives students the opportunity to try their hand at translating the passage. This exercise in translation reinforces the idea that translation is more than simply knowing the meaning of individual words; it involves knowing how grammatical structures function and how words relate to one another within a sentence. It also involves making choices between different possible translations for individual words and phrases and hence always includes a degree of interpretation. It is important to convey to students the idea that there is no single correct translation and that, in fact, much of Torah commentary arises from the fact that the same word or phrase may legitimately be understood in more than one way.

Torah Translations

To enable students to appreciate the variety of different possible translations that can exist even for a short Torah Study Text, four different translations of each Torah Study Text are provided, reflecting slightly different approaches to the text. In the chapter notes, this Teacher's Guide points out examples of variation among our four translations for each Torah Study Text.

The first translation, from the Jewish Publication Society in 1999, renders the Hebrew in a contemporary English idiom. This was the translation favored by the Reform Movement at the time that *Bet Is for B'reishit* and *Tav Is for Torah* were originally published; an earlier version of this translation, from 1967, appears in *The Torah: A Modern Commentary*, published by UAHC Press. The second translation is from the ArtScroll *Chumash*, a publication with a traditional, as opposed to liberal, orientation. This orientation is reflected, among other things, in the use of the word *HaShem* to translate the four-letter name of God. The third translation, by Everett Fox, is a contemporary scholarly version that attempts to preserve the terse and often poetic literary style of the Hebrew text in the English rendition. The last selection, the *Jerusalem Bible* translation from 1969, is the oldest and tends toward literal as opposed to idiomatic translations. It is also the only one that uses archaic language (e.g., "Thou art" instead of "You are").

Since the original publication of *Bet Is for B'reishit* and *Tav Is for Torah*, URJ Press has published *The Torah: A Modern Commentary*, revised edition. This work, the new standard for the Reform Movement, includes a gender-sensitive translation. Although translations from *The Torah: A Modern Commentary*, revised edition are not included in *Bet Is for B'reishit* and *Tav Is for Torah*, you might want to share some of them with your class. Notes explaining the translation decisions for this work can be found at www.urjbooksandmusic.com.

Vocabulary

The first chapter of each unit introduces the vocabulary words for that unit. Vocabulary words are derived from the Torah Study Text and have been selected because of the frequency with which they appear in Hebrew literature. With very few exceptions, these words appear 100 times or more in the Bible. Some appear over 500 times.

The vocabulary for each unit has been limited to between five and eight words, with the recognition that memorization is difficult for many adult learners. It is not essential for students to attain an active knowledge of these words (i.e., the ability to produce them when asked, "How do you say *word* in Hebrew?"), but it is necessary for them to develop a passive knowledge of them (i.e., the ability to recognize these words when they appear in a Hebrew passage). The words presented as vocabulary in each unit appear in the exercises of both chapters of that unit and in subsequent units. Many also reappear in the Torah Study Texts of subsequent chapters.

Hebrew Roots

The first chapter of each unit also introduces two new Hebrew roots, both of which appear in some form in the Torah Study Text. As with the vocabulary words, the roots have been chosen because of the frequency with which they appear in the Bible and Hebrew literature. It is important that students become able to recognize these roots, as they appear in the exercises of both chapters of that unit and in subsequent units. Many also reappear in subsequent Torah Study Texts.

To aid students in developing the ability to recognize a Hebrew root within a word, a list is provided for each root of classical and/or modern Hebrew words derived from that root. These words are included for enrichment only. Students are not expected to memorize these words.

Torah Commentary

Three to five commentaries on different words or phrases within the Torah Study Text are presented, drawn from a wide range of traditional and contemporary sources. The selections have been chosen not only to reflect the variety of approaches to Torah study, but more importantly, because each selection uses some aspect of the Hebrew as its point of departure. Providing our students the opportunity to explore details in the Hebrew that may be obscured in an English translation enables them to experience firsthand the intellectual creativity of the Jewish practice of Torah study.

Exercises

The exercises following the first chapter of each unit are primarily intended to aid the student in learning the new vocabulary and roots introduced in that chapter, as this material will recur in the second chapter of the unit and in subsequent chapters. These exercises also review some material introduced previously. The exercises are probably most effective as homework, providing students with an opportunity for additional practice and reinforcement outside of class. Prior to beginning the second chapter of each unit, teachers may choose to utilize some of these exercises in class as review. It may be helpful for teachers to remind students that the learning of the new vocabulary and roots is the primary goal; completion of the exercises is secondary, intended mainly to reinforce that goal.

Both script and block print forms of the Hebrew letters were introduced in *Aleph Isn't Tough*. Students can choose the form of the Hebrew they prefer to use in writing their answers to the excercises.

Extra Credit

As in *Aleph Isn't Enough*, the first chapter of each unit concludes with an Extra Credit section, exploring various topics connected with Jewish religious life and practice, often derived from or related to the Torah Study Text. Such topics include Jewish time, the classical commentator Rashi, modern Hebrew poetry utilizing biblical characters, talmudic passages expanding upon biblical verses, and Jewish skills such as reading Torah or interpreting layers of meaning in a text. As its name implies, this material is supplemental, intended for the students' enrichment and enjoyment.

The second chapter of each unit includes the following sections.

Torah Study Text: Vocabulary and Root Review

The second chapter of each unit begins with a reprinting of that unit's Torah Study Text, with the new vocabulary words and roots from the first chapter highlighted. Again, this is not intended as an exercise in developing reading fluency. The Torah Study Text is included here for review: to provide students with the opportunity to revisit the new vocabulary words and roots in the context of a now somewhat more familiar text. Many adult learners find it difficult to memorize and retain vocabulary; review and repetition can assist in this process.

Building Blocks

The second chapter of each unit introduces two or three basic Hebrew grammatical concepts, called Building Blocks. The following ideas underlie the presentation of Building Blocks:

1. Grammatical concepts are presented simply and clearly, avoiding as much as possible the use of technical terminology.

2. To keep the amount of required memorization to a minimum, only those grammatical forms that appear frequently in prayer book and biblical Hebrew are introduced. In general, individual grammatical forms are introduced rather than complete paradigms. Complete paradigms

for verbs, however, are included in the verb charts at the back of the book.

3. As in *Aleph Isn't Enough*, the grammatical concepts introduced are those that enable students to determine the composition of a word (its base structure with the addition of prefixes and suffixes) and how the words in a passage relate to one another (e.g., demonstratives, possession). Most of the Building Blocks introduced in *Bet Is for B'reishit* and *Tav Is for Torah* are verbal prefixes and suffixes and pronoun endings. Other types of prefixes, such as the reversing *vav* and the question הַ are also introduced, as well as the concept of different verb patterns (הִפְעִיל ,פִּעֵל ,פָּעַל).

4. The material presented in each chapter is progressive, building upon the concepts introduced in prior chapters. Therefore, it is important that students understand the grammatical concepts introduced in each chapter before moving on to learn new material.

Torah Study Text with Building Blocks

Aspects of the grammatical concepts introduced in the chapter are illustrated in the unit's Torah Study Text. After being introduced to the new Building Blocks, students revisit the Torah Study Text with the Building Blocks highlighted, providing them another opportunity to review the text and to see the grammar concepts in context.

Grammar Enrichment

This section presents additional grammatical information beyond what is introduced in the main body of the chapter. In most cases, it consists of a chart showing newly introduced verb forms for several or all roots already learned. In a few cases, it provides an explanation of a grammatical detail encountered within the unit's Torah Study Text (such as the הַ ending meaning "toward"). The material in the Grammar Enrichment section is intended for reinforcement of learning, but not for memorization.

Additional Reading and Translation Practice

This section may be done in class or for reinforcement of learning at home. It contains Hebrew excerpts from the prayer book, Haggadah, Jewish home rituals, and biblical passages that illustrate new vocabulary words, roots, and/or grammatical concepts introduced in that unit. Most of these excerpts will be familiar to those who are already active participants in Jewish life and can provide an introduction to some well-known Hebrew passages for those who are new to or unfamiliar with Jewish religious practice.

In some cases, it may be helpful to locate these passages for students in the prayer book and even, perhaps, to sing them with the melody most commonly used in your community. Page numbers where these passages can be found in Reform publications are indicated in the chapter notes of this Teacher's Guide.

It may also be helpful to remind students as they begin their attempt at translation that the Glossary at the back of the book contains all the vocabulary and roots introduced in the current textbook and in the prior volumes in this series.

Translations

The translations that immediately follow the Hebrew excerpts are not provided in idiomatic English. Rather, they are as close to literal as possible, to enable students to see multiple meaning of individual words within the text and a variety of possible ways to translate those words.

Exercises

Since the Additional Reading and Translation Practice can also serve as homework or reinforcement exercises, the second chapter of each unit contains only two or three additional exercises. All the new vocabulary words and roots introduced in the first chapter of the unit appear in the exercises of the second. The first one or two exercises reinforce the learning of the new grammatical structures and, in many cases, also provide a review of Hebrew roots. The last exercise is a series of sentences for translation, with a repetitive format and changes from line to line that enable students to review grammatical structures, vocabulary, and roots.

As in *Aleph Isn't Enough*, none of the exercises require students to generate or produce Hebrew passages on their own by translating from English into Hebrew. The focus is entirely on developing the students' ability to recognize familiar words and grammatical structures in the Hebrew and to translate from Hebrew into English.

From Our Texts

This section is included in *Tav Is for Torah* only. It contains a passage from postbiblical Hebrew literature (such as the Mishnah, the songs "Ani Maamin" and "Hava Nagila," modern Hebrew poetry) that illustrates a new grammatical structure, vocabulary, or root introduced in that unit. This passage is not intended as translation practice for students, as the Hebrew is generally too lengthy or complex. It is included for the students' enrichment and enjoyment.

Scope and Sequence

Following is an outline of the basic material introduced in each chapter.

Bet Is for B'reishit – Book 3

Unit 1: Torah Study Text: Genesis 1:1–5
Chapter 1

1. Vocabulary:

   חֹשֶׁךְ פָּנִים רוּחַ מַיִם אוֹר בֵּין עֶרֶב בֹּקֶר

2. Hebrew Roots: ה־י־ה and א־מ־ר

3. Torah Commentary:

   a. The Torah begins not with בַּרֵאשִׁית, "in the beginning," but with בְּרֵאשִׁית, "in beginning" or "in a beginning."—R' Bunim of Pshischa

   b. The Torah begins with the letter ב, the second letter of the Hebrew alphabet.— Horav Dovid Shneur

   c. The Torah states וַיְהִי־עֶרֶב, "and there was evening," without ever stating יְהִי־עֶרֶב, "let there be evening."—*B'reishit Rabbah* 3:7

4. Extra Credit: A Day in Jewish Time

Unit 1: Torah Study Text: Genesis 1:1–5
Chapter 2

1. Building Blocks:

   a. Perfect verbs: הוּא form

   b. Imperfect verbs: הוּא form (the י prefix)

   c. Reversing *vav*

2. Grammar Enrichment: chart of participle, perfect, and imperfect הוּא forms

3. Additional Reading and Translation Practice:

   a. עוֹשֶׂה שָׁלוֹם

   b. From אֲדוֹן עוֹלָם

   c. From the Torah service (from Psalm 10:16; Psalm 93:1; and Exodus 15:18)

   d. וְנֶאֱמַר (Zechariah 14:9)

   e. Blessing for sons (from Genesis 48:20) and daughters

   f. Genesis 2:1–3

Unit 2: Torah Study Text: Genesis 4:1–5, 8–10
Chapter 3

1. Vocabulary:

אָדָם אִשָׁה אָח אֶל לֹא קוֹל דָם

2. Hebrew Roots: יְ־דְ־עַ and עְ־בְ־דְ

3. Building Blocks:

   a. More on the reversing *vav*

   b. The preposition אֶת

4. Torah Commentary:

   a. Verse 1 begins וְהָאָדָם יָדַע, without a reversing *vav*.—Rashi on Genesis 4:1

   b. The word אֶת is regarded as the preposition "with."—*B'reishit Rabbah* 22:3

   c. In verse 10, the plural word-pair form דְמֵי, "bloods of," appears.—*B'reishit Rabbah* 22:21 and *Mishnah Sanhedrin* 4:5; BT *Sanhedrin* 37a

5. Extra Credit: A Modern Poem with a Biblical Theme: "Written in pencil in the sealed freight car"

Unit 2: Torah Study Text: Genesis 4:1–5, 8–10
Chapter 4

1. Building Blocks:

   a. Feminine perfect verbs: הִיא form (the ה ending)

   b. Feminine imperfect verbs: הִיא form (the ת prefix)

   c. The question ה

2. Grammar Enrichment: chart of feminine participle, perfect, and imperfect הִיא forms

3. Additional Reading and Translation Practice:

   a. From Genesis 1:2

   b. Psalm 150:6

   c. From נִשְׁמַת כָּל חַי

   d. From הַתִּקְוָה

   e. From Genesis 3:6

   f. From Proverbs 6:20, 22, 23

Unit 3: Torah Study Text: Genesis 11:1–9

Chapter 5

1. Vocabulary:

אֶחָד אַחַת רֵעַ אֶבֶן עִיר רֹאשׁ שֵׁם

2. Hebrew Roots: ב־נ־ה י־שׁ־ב and

3. Torah Commentary:

   a. Those who are building the tower are called בְּנֵי הָאָדָם, "the children of Adam/humankind."—Rashi on Genesis 11:5 and R' Zvi Natan Finkel, the elder of Slobodka

   b. It is twice stated that God scattered the people.—Rashi on Genesis 11:8–9

4. Extra Credit: Rashi

Unit 3: Torah Study Text: Genesis 11:1–9

Chapter 6

1. Building Blocks:

   a. Plural perfect verb forms (the וּ ending)

   b. Plural imperfect verb forms (the וּ ending and יִ prefix)

   c. the pronoun endings כֶם and הֶם

2. Grammar Enrichment: chart of masculine plural participle, perfect, and imperfect forms

3. Additional Reading and Translation Practice:

   a. From וְשָׁמְרוּ (Exodus 31:16)

   b. From אַשְׁרֵי (Psalm 84:5)

   c. From בִּרְכַּת הַמָּזוֹן

   d. Psalm 118:1–4

   e. From יִשְׂמְחוּ

   f. From Isaiah 2:2–4

Unit 4: Torah Study Text: Genesis 12:1–7

Chapter 7

1. Vocabulary:

שָׁנָה כְּנַעַן עַד מָקוֹם אָז זֶרַע

2. Hebrew Roots: review of ק־ד־שׁ, ה־ל־ל, ד־ב־ר, ב־ר־ךְ, ח־י־ה and צ־ו־ה

3. Torah Commentary:

a. Why does the word לְךָ appear in the command לֶךְ לְךָ?—Avivah Gottlieb Zornberg

b. Song by Debbie Friedman

c. Why are three different point of departure mentioned in verse 1?—Richard Elliott Friedman

d. In verse 3, מְבָרְכֶיךָ, "those who bless you," is plural, while מְקַלֶּלְךָ, "he who curses you," is singular.—Ralbag

e. The phrase at the end of verse 3, וְנִבְרְכוּ בְךָ, can be understood in various ways.—Richard Elliott Friedman

4. Extra Credit: Preparing a Torah Reading (using a *tikkun*)

Unit 4: Torah Study Text: Genesis 12:1–7
Chapter 8

1. Building Blocks:

   a. Hebrew verb patterns: the פָּעַל pattern

   b. Perfect and imperfect הוּא, הִיא, and הֵם forms in the פָּעַל pattern

2. Grammar Enrichment: chart of perfect and imperfect הוּא, הִיא, and הֵם forms in the פָּעַל pattern

3. Additional Reading and Translation Practice:

   a. Shabbat candle lighting blessing

   b. From מִי שֶׁבֵּרַךְ

   c. From בְּרֹאשׁ הַשָּׁנָה

   d. Words to mourners

   e. Psalm 148:13–14

   f. Numbers 6:22–23 and 24–26 (Priestly Benediction)

   g. From אַשְׁרֵי (Psalm 145:9–11, 21 and Psalm 115:18)

Unit 5: Torah Study Text: Genesis 22:1–5, 9–12
Chapter 9

1. Vocabulary:

   הִנֵּה הַר עִם עֵץ עַיִן נַעַר

2. Hebrew Roots: ע־ל־ה and ה־ל־ך

3. Torah Commentary:

   a. The word דְּבָרִים can mean either "things" or "words."—*Tanchuma, Vayeira* 18

b. The verb הַעֲלֵהוּ in verse 2 could be understood simply as "bring him up."—Rashi on Genesis 22:2

c. Bob Dylan song

d. The word הַמָּקוֹם in verse 4 can mean both "the place" and "the One who is in all places."—R' Avraham of Sochachew

e. Why does it state in verse 3: וַיַּשְׁכֵּם אַבְרָהָם בַּבֹּקֶר, "Abraham rose early in the morning"?—*Tanchuma, Vayeira* 22

4. Extra Credit: The *Akeidah* and Rosh HaShanah

Unit 5: Torah Study Text: Genesis 22:1–5, 9–12

Chapter 10

1. Building Blocks:

   a. Hebrew verb patterns: the הִפְעִיל pattern

   b. Participle, perfect, and imperfect הוּא, הִיא, and הֵם forms in the הִפְעִיל pattern

   c. Variations on the הִפְעִיל pattern: הַמּוֹצִיא

2. Grammar Enrichment: chart of participle, perfect, and imperfect הוּא forms in the הִפְעִיל pattern

3. Additional Reading and Translation Practice:

   a. שֶׁהֶחֱיָנוּ

   b. Isaiah 52:7

   c. From the קְדֻשָּׁה

   d. From the קִדּוּשׁ לְעֶרֶב שַׁבָּת

   e. הַבְדָּלָה blessing

   f. Genesis 1:4

   g. From מַעֲרִיב עֲרָבִים

Tav Is for Torah – Book 4

Unit 1: Torah Study Text: Genesis 28:10–17
Chapter 1

1. Vocabulary:

זֶה זֹאת אֵלֶּה אֲנִי אָנֹכִי יַם יֵשׁ

2. Hebrew Roots: י־ר־א and ל־ק־ח

3. Torah Commentary:

   a. The words וַיִּפְגַּע בַּמָּקוֹם, "and he encountered the place," in verse 11, can be understood in different ways.—Avivah Gottlieb Zornberg

   b. The sequence of the verbs עֹלִים וְיֹרְדִים, "ascending and descending," in verse 12—Lawrence Kushner

   c. The word עָלָיו in verse 13 is ambiguous.—*B'reishit Rabbah* 69:3

   d. At the end of verse 17, Jacob proclaims וְזֶה שַׁעַר הַשָּׁמָיִם.—R' Menahem Mendl of Kotzk

4. Extra Credit: The Patriarchs and Daily Prayer

Unit 1: Torah Study Text: Genesis 28:10–17
Chapter 2

1. Building Blocks:
   a. This and these: זֶה and זֹאת and אֵלֶּה
   b. That and those: הַהוּא and הַהִיא and הַהֵם (second Chanukah candle lighting blessing)

2. Grammar Enrichment: ה meaning "toward"

3. Additional Reading and Translation Practice:

   a. שֶׁהֶחֱיָנוּ
   b. From the Passover Four Questions
   c. וְזֹאת הַתּוֹרָה
   d. וְנֶאֱמַר
   e. from Deuteronomy 1:1
   f. מִי כָמֹכָה
   g. From the Blessing after the Haftarah

4. From Hebrew Literature: *Mishnah Pe-ah* 1:1

Unit 2: Torah Study Text: Exodus 3:1–7

Chapter 3

1. Vocabulary:

    כִּי כֹּהֵן אַחַר מִדְבָּר אֵשׁ תּוֹךְ

2. Hebrew Roots: ר־א־ה and ב־ו־א

3. Torah Commentary:

    a. Verse 2 states וַיַּרְא, "and he saw," but there is no object for the verb וַיַּרְא.—Lawrence Kushner

    b. The words אָסֻרָה־נָּא, "let me/I will turn aside now," in verse 3 are somewhat superfluous.—Rabbi A. L. Scheinbaum

    c. Why are the words אֲשֶׁר אַתָּה עוֹמֵד, "that you are standing," specified in verse 5?—*Beginning the Journey: A Women's Commentary on the Torah*

4. Extra Credit: Layers of Meaning in Torah Study (entering the פַּרְדֵּס)

Unit 2: Torah Study Text: Exodus 3:1–7

Chapter 4

1. Building Blocks:

    a. אֲנִי or אָנֹכִי perfect verb forms (the תִּי ending)

    b. אֲנִי or אָנֹכִי imperfect verb forms (the א prefix)

    c. The pronoun endings ִי and ַי and נִי

2. Grammar Enrichment: chart of אֲנִי or אָנֹכִי ("I") perfect and imperfect forms

3. Additional Reading and Translation Practice:

    a. Psalm 23:1

    b. כִּי אֶשְׁמְרָה שַׁבָּת

    c. From Psalm 121:1–2

    d. From *Havdalah* (Isaiah 12:2)

    e. From אֲדוֹן עוֹלָם

    f. Exodus 3:13, 3:14, various translations of אֶהְיֶה אֲשֶׁר אֶהְיֶה

4. From Hebrew Literature: "Ani Maamin"

Unit 3: Torah Study Text: Leviticus 19:1–4, 15–17, 33–34
Chapter 5

1. Vocabulary words:

   אֵל עֵדָה מִשְׁפָּט גֵּר חֵטְא לֵאמֹר

2. Hebrew Roots: נ־שׂ־א ע־מ־ד and

3. Torah Commentary:

   a. The phrase אֲנִי יְהוָֹה אֱלֹהֵיכֶם, "I am the Eternal your God," is repeated at the end of verses 2, 3, and 4.—Rabbi Abraham J. Twerski, M.D.

   b. A broader meaning for the phrase לֹא־תַעֲשׂוּ עָוֶל בַּמִּשְׁפָּט, "you shall not do injustice/unrighteousness in justice/judgment/law," in verse 15—R' Simhah Bunim of Pshischa

   c. The connection between the first and second part of verse 17—R' Yehudah Leib, the Mokhi'ah of Polonnoye

   d. The plural ending כֶם on the word אֱלֹהֵיכֶם, "your God," in verse 34—Rashi on Leviticus 19:34

4. Extra Credit: All the Rest Is Commentary (BT *Shabbat* 31a)

Unit 3: Torah Study Text: Leviticus 19:1–4, 15–17, 33–34
Chapter 6

1. Building Blocks:

   a. "You" singular and plural perfect verb forms (the תָ and תֶם endings)

   b. "You" singular and plural imperfect verb forms (the תְ prefix and וּ ending)

2. Grammar Enrichment: chart of "you" masculine, singular and plural, perfect and imperfect forms

3. Additional Reading and Translation Practice:

   a. From Psalm 121:1–2

   b. עַל שְׁלֹשָׁה דְבָרִים

   c. לְמַעַן תִּזְכְּרוּ (Numbers 15:40–41)

   d. From the Shabbat evening קִדּוּשׁ

   e. Deuteronomy 4:39 (included in the עָלֵינוּ)

   f. From the בִּרְכַּת הַמָּזוֹן

   g. Leviticus 25:10

4. From Hebrew Literature: "Instead of a Love Poem" by Yehuda Amichai

Unit 4: Torah Study Text: Deuteronomy 5:6–7, 12–18

Chapter 7

1. Vocabulary:

אַחֵר כַּאֲשֶׁר בַּת שַׁעַר לְמַעַן מְלָאכָה

2. Hebrew Roots: נ־ו־ח and כ־ב־ד

3. Torah Commentary:

   a. The words עַל פָּנָי at the end of verse 7—Rashi on Deuteronomy 5:7

   b. Verse 15 links the remembrance of slavery in Egypt with God's commandment לַעֲשׂוֹת, "to make," the Sabbath.—Rabbi Abraham J. Twerski, M.D.

   c. The wording of the commandment לֹא תִרְצָח, "you shall not murder," as a general statement—*Torah Gems*, compiled by Aharon Yaakov Greenberg

   d. Chasidic teaching related to the author by Rabbi Sholom Brodt, who received it from Rabbi Shlomo Carlebach

4. Extra Credit: The Fourth Commandment

Unit 4: Torah Study Text: Deuteronomy 5:6–7, 12–18

Chapter 8

1. Building Blocks:

   a. "Have" and "not have" in Hebrew

   b. "Have" and "not have" in the perfect and imperfect

2. Grammar Enrichment: אֲשֶׁר, "that/who/which," used with the preposition ל to indicate possession

3. Additional Reading and Translation Practice:

   a. From יוֹם זֶה לְיִשְׂרָאֵל

   b. From אֲדוֹן עוֹלָם

   c. לְךָ יְיָ (I Chronicles 29:11)

   d. From יִגְדַּל

   e. From אֱמֶת וְיַצִּיב

   f. I Samuel 1:1–2

4. From Hebrew Literature: "Every Man Has a Name" by Zelda Mishkovsky

Unit 5: Torah Study Text: Deuteronomy 30:11–16, 19
Chapter 9

1. Vocabulary:

   הַיּוֹם קָרוֹב לִפְנֵי מָוֶת רַע

2. Hebrew Roots: ע־ב־ר and מ־ו־ת

3. Torah Commentary:

   a. The extra nuance added by the inclusion of the word לַעֲשׂתוֹ at the end of verse 14 —R. Menahem Mendl of Kotsk

   b. The word הַיּוֹם, "today," is stated in both verses 15 and 19.—Rabbi Moshe Feinstein

   c. The verb וּבָחַרְתָּ, "choose," in verse 19—the Mirrer Mashgiach, Horav Yechezkel Levinstein

4. Extra Credit: "Not in Heaven" (BT, *Bava M'tzia* 59b)

Unit 5: Torah Study Text: Deuteronomy 30:11–16, 19
Chapter 10

1. Building Blocks:

   a. אָנוּ or אֲנַחְנוּ perfect verb forms (the נוּ ending)

   b. אָנוּ or אֲנַחְנוּ imperfect verb forms (the נ prefix)

2. Grammar Enrichment: chart of אָנוּ or אֲנַחְנוּ ("we") perfect and imperfect forms

3. An Additional Note on Hebrew Verb Patterns: the נִפְעַל pattern

4. Additional Reading and Translation Practice:

   a. From גְּבוּרוֹת

   b. From the קְדוּשָׁה

   c. עֲבָדִים הָיִינוּ

   d. Psalm 137:1

   e. Psalm 118:26

   f. From בִּרְכַּת הַמָּזוֹן

5. From Hebrew Literature: "Hava Nagila"

6. A Concluding Thought: BT, *Taanit* 7a

Notes on

Bet Is for B'reishit – Book 3

Before You Begin

It is encouraging to students to begin on a warm, welcoming note. Congratulate your students on their achievements in Hebrew learning thus far. Since the book that they are about to begin is organized around Torah Study Texts and they are about to study their first Torah passage in Hebrew, you may wish to begin with the blessing for Torah study, which can be found in the gender-sensitive *Gates of Prayer* on page 12:

בָּרוּךְ אַתָּה יְיָ אֱלֹהֵינוּ מֶלֶךְ הָעוֹלָם, אֲשֶׁר קִדְּשָׁנוּ בְּמִצְוֹתָיו,
וְצִוָּנוּ לַעֲסוֹק בְּדִבְרֵי תוֹרָה:

Blessed are You, Eternal our God, Sovereign of the universe, who has made us holy with {His} mitzvot and has commanded us to occupy ourselves with words of Torah.

Each chapter of this book includes a variety of different learning activities. Some of the information may best be presented lecture-style by the teacher, but other learning may more effectively be accomplished by the students working through material themselves, either individually or in *chevruta*, cooperative learning pairs. For those students who may be new to *chevruta* study, explain that this is the traditional Jewish method of engaging in text study. Working in pairs enables students to assist one another and also helps both students remain focused on the task together. It also provides an opportunity for students to become better acquainted with one another. The teacher can circulate among the various groups, providing additional commentary and assistance as needed. Students should feel free to choose new partners in subsequent class sessions or remain with the same one.

Torah Study Text: Genesis 1:1–5 [page 1]

You may choose to have your students do this opening activity in *chevruta*, cooperative learning pairs. As indicated in the introduction, this opening activity is not designed as a Hebrew Reading Practice, but as Torah Text Study. It is not necessary for students to work on achieving fluency in reading this Torah passage aloud, as it is generally not read aloud in Hebrew as a community in any

Jewish prayer service or ritual. Rather, this opening activity provides students with an opportunity to examine an unfamiliar Hebrew passage and pick out the elements that they have learned and can recognize.

Reassure your students that much of the material in this passage is new and they are not expected to know it. Similarly, they may not be able to recall all the material that was introduced in *Aleph Isn't Enough,* as adult learners often have difficulty with memorization and retention. Whatever they can identify is wonderful. As they progress, more and more Hebrew will become familiar to them.

Following are all the words, roots, endings, and prefixes appearing in Genesis 1:1–5 that were introduced in *Aleph Isn't Enough.* The chapter where they were introduced is indicated in parentheses.

בְּרֵאשִׁית֤ בָּרָא אֱלֹהִים אֵת הַשָּׁמַיִם וְאֵת הָאָרֶץ: ²וְהָאָרֶץ הָיְתָה תֹהוּ וָבֹהוּ וְחֹשֶׁךְ עַל־פְּנֵי תְהוֹם וְרוּחַ אֱלֹהִים מְרַחֶפֶת עַל־פְּנֵי הַמָּיִם: ³וַיֹּאמֶר אֱלֹהִים יְהִי אוֹר וַיְהִי־אוֹר: ⁴וַיַּרְא אֱלֹהִים אֶת־הָאוֹר כִּי־טוֹב וַיַּבְדֵּל אֱלֹהִים בֵּין הָאוֹר וּבֵין הַחֹשֶׁךְ: ⁵וַיִּקְרָא אֱלֹהִים לָאוֹר יוֹם וְלַחֹשֶׁךְ קָרָא לָיְלָה וַיְהִי־עֶרֶב וַיְהִי־בֹקֶר יוֹם אֶחָד:

in [the] beginning (A.I.E. Ch 8)	—	בְּרֵאשִׁית

(see note on this word in "Translating the Torah Study Text" below)

create (A.I.E. Ch 3)	—	ב־ר־א
God (A.I.E. Ch 4), appears six times in our Torah Study Text		אֱלֹהִים

definite direct object marker (untranslatable) (A.I.E. Ch 4), appears three
  times in our Torah Study Text   —   אֵת, אֶת

the (attached prefix) (A.I.E. Ch 1), appears on the
  following words: —   הַ, הָ

הַשָּׁמַיִם, הָאָרֶץ, וְהָאָרֶץ, הַמָּיִם, הָאוֹר, הַחֹשֶׁךְ

heavens, sky *m* (A.I.E. Ch 3)	—	שָׁמַיִם

and (attached prefix) (A.I.E. Ch 2), appears on the
  following words: —   וְ, וָ, וּ:

וְאֵת, וְהָאָרֶץ, וָבֹהוּ, וְחֹשֶׁךְ, וְרוּחַ, וּבֵין, וְלַחֹשֶׁךְ

the vav on the following words is a reversing vav (to be introduced in the next chapter), though it can also be translated as and:

וַיֹּאמֶר, וַיְהִי, וַיַּרְא, וַיַּבְדֵּל, וַיִּקְרָא

earth, land *f (A.I.E. Ch 3)* (אֶרֶץ *becomes* אָרֶץ *when the prefix* הָ, *the, is attached*) — אֶרֶץ

on, about *(A.I.E. Ch 8), appears twice in our Torah Study Text* — עַל

good *adj (A.I.E. Ch 5)* — טוֹב

to, for *(attached preposition) (A.I.E. Ch 8)* — ־לְ

(with the vowels לַ *or* לָ *it means to the, for the); appears on the following words:* לָאוֹר, וְלַחֹשֶׁךְ

day *m (A.I.E. Ch 3), appears two times in our Torah Study Text* — יוֹם

night *m (A.I.E. Ch 2)* — לַיְלָה

Translating the Torah Study Text [pages 1–3]

You may choose to have your students work individually on their own translations or in *chevruta*, learning pairs. Remind your students that there is no single correct translation. Every translation is an interpretation, and there are often several possible ways that a given verse, or even a single word, can be understood. You might illustrate this point with the very first word of the Torah, before having the students begin working on their own translations. There are several possibilities to consider when attempting to translate the word בְּרֵאשִׁית:

1. The attached prefix בְּ can be translated in many different ways. Here it is possible to translate it as "in," "with," or even "at."

2. The vowel on the prefix is בְּ and not בַּ, meaning that it does NOT include the word "the."

   This detail gives rise to the first Torah commentary included in the Torah Commentary section of this chapter.

3. The word רֵאשִׁית itself can be translated as the noun "beginning," as does the *Jerusalem Bible* (the fourth and oldest translation cited in our chapter), which also inserts in the English the word "the," which does not appear in the Hebrew: "In *the* beginning." But the word רֵאשִׁית is more often used in the Bible as a word-pair form: "beginning of." This is the interpretation favored by the more recent translations included in our chapter. If בְּרֵאשִׁית is understood as a word-pair form ("in/with/at [the] beginning of"), the obvious question is, what is the second word of the word pair? Since Torah scrolls are written without vowels, it is possible that the word following

בְּרֵאשִׁית should be interpreted not as בָּרָא, "[he] created," but as בְּרָא, "creating," yielding the translation: "In/at beginning of creating of God [i.e., God's creating]."

As your students work on their translations, the following reminders may assist them:

1. The subject often comes after the verb in classical Hebrew, as in verse 1: בָּרָא אֱלֹהִים, "God created."

2. Sometimes no form of the verb "to be" appears in the Hebrew and must be inserted in the English translation, as in verse 4: וַיַּרְא אֱלֹהִים אֶת־הָאוֹר כִּי־טוֹב, "and God saw the light that [was] good."

3. Sometimes an additional word may need to be inserted into the translation to make it sound smooth in English, as in verse 4: וַיַּרְא אֱלֹהִים אֶת־הָאוֹר כִּי־טוֹב, "and God saw the light that [it] [was] good," or in verse 3: יְהִי־אוֹר, "let [there] be light or let light be."

4. Prepositions do not always translate smoothly from one language to another. Sometimes they may best be left untranslated, as in verse 5: וַיִּקְרָא אֱלֹהִים לָאוֹר יוֹם, "and God called {to} the light day."

[pages 3–4]

The four Torah translations provided all take slightly different approaches to the text. You may wish to point out to your students how some of the issues in translation mentioned above are handled differently by the various translators:

1. Verse 4: וַיַּרְא אֱלֹהִים אֶת־הָאוֹר כִּי־טוֹב: "God saw that the light was good" versus "God saw the light: that it was good."

2. Verse 5: וַיִּקְרָא אֱלֹהִים לָאוֹר יוֹם: "God called the light Day" versus God "called to the light: 'Day.'"

You may also wish to provide your students with a brief explanation of the orientation of each of these translations, as the same four will be used throughout *Bet Is for B'reishit* and *Tav Is for Torah*.

The first translation, from the Jewish Publication Society in 1999, renders the Hebrew in a contemporary English idiom. This is the translation favored by the Reform movement; an earlier version of this translation, from 1967, appears in *The Torah: A Modern Commentary*, published by UAHC Press. Notice that this is the only one of our four translations that renders the first word of the Torah not as "in the beginning" or "at the beginning," but "when God began."

The second translation is from the ArtScroll *Chumash*, a publication with a traditional, as opposed to liberal, orientation. Notice how only this translation renders the word pair רוּחַ אֱלֹהִים in verse 2 as "the Divine Presence." Also notice how this translation uses both idiomatic language, as in verse 2, "when the earth was astonishingly empty," as well as very literal language, such as in translating the prepositions in verse 4, "God separated *between* the light and the darkness" and in verse 5, "God called *to* the light: 'Day,' and *to* the darkness He called: 'Night.'"

The third translation, by Everett Fox, is a contemporary scholarly version that attempts to preserve the terse but often poetic literary style of the Hebrew text in the English rendition. Notice the way that Fox sets up his translation, not in prose paragraphs but almost as a poetic structure, and uses poetic language such as "wild and waste" in verse 2 or "There was setting, there was dawning" in verse 5.

The last selection, the *Jerusalem Bible* translation from 1969, is the oldest and tends toward literal as opposed to idiomatic translations. It is the only one that translates the first word בְּרֵאשִׁית as a noun, not part of a word pair: "In the beginning God created."

Vocabulary [pages 4–5]

After introducing the vocabulary words, you may wish to give your students time in *chevruta*, cooperative learning pairs, to practice reading the words aloud and to locate the words within the Torah Study Text. Remind your students that the words introduced in the Vocabulary section are words that appear very frequently in the Bible and classical Hebrew texts and will recur in subsequent chapters of this book. Encourage your students to learn these words to the best of their ability. There will be no new vocabulary words introduced in the second chapter of each unit.

All the new vocabulary words are highlighted within the Torah Study Text at the beginning of Chapter 2, on pages 1–12. The word פָּנִים, "face/faces/surface," appears only in word-pair form in the Torah Study Text, in verse 2: פְּנֵי הַמָּיִם and פְּנֵי תְהוֹם.

Some additional notes on the vocabulary:

1. The words פָּנִים, "face/faces/surface," and רוּחַ, "wind/spirit," are sometimes treated as masculine and sometimes feminine.

2. When the word בֵּין means "between," it is generally repeated in the Hebrew, though not in the English translation. We see this in verse 4: בֵּין הָאוֹר וּבֵין הַחֹשֶׁךְ, "between the light and {between} the darkness." This repetition of the word בֵּין can also be seen in the first verse of *V'shamru*, included in the Shabbat evening liturgy in the gender-sensitive *Gates of Prayer* on page 55: בֵּינִי וּבֵין בְּנֵי יִשְׂרָאֵל, "between Me and {between} the Children of Israel." The word בֵּינִי is also an example of the use

of בֵּין with an attached pronoun ending. The word בֵּין can, however, mean "between" without repeating in the Hebrew. Sometimes בֵּין appears in the phrase בֵּין X לְ Y, where the prefix is translated into English as "and." This occurs in the Havdalah blessing הַמַּבְדִּיל בֵּין קֹדֶשׁ לְחוֹל, בֵּין אוֹר לְחֹשֶׁךְ, *who makes a distinction between sacred and profane, between light and darkness.*

The Hebrew Root [pages 5–6]

In this section, all the places where each root appears in the Torah Study Text are listed. You may wish to give your students time to go back to the Hebrew paragraph at the beginning of the chapter and locate the roots there.

Inform your students that the two Hebrew roots introduced in each unit have been selected because they appear very frequently in the Bible and classical Hebrew texts. They will recur in subsequent chapters of this book. Encourage your students to learn these words to the best of their ability.There will be no new roots introduced in the second chapter of each unit.

Remind your students that, as in *Aleph Isn't Enough*, the ancient and modern words derived from the roots that are included in this section are for enrichment only. They illustrate the various ways that roots can appear within a word, with different vowels and prefixes and suffixes surrounding the root letters, and the possible disappearance, as in the root ה־י־ה, of a root letter. Students do not need to memorize these words.

We have presented the view that there is no participle form of the root ה־י־ה. See the note in this Teacher's Guide on page 33 on אֲדוֹן עוֹלָם—item 2 in the Additional Reading and Translation Practice section of this chapter.

Torah Commentary [page 6]

This section provides students with a taste of Hebrew Torah study. You may decide to go over this section with the entire class as a group or have your students look over this material in *chevruta*, learning pairs. These commentaries all stem from some detail in the Hebrew that would not necessarily be apparent in an English translation. It may be helpful to your students to refer back to the Hebrew of the Torah Study Text at the beginning of the chapter to locate the context for each commentary.

A note on the grammar of the third commentary: The *vav* on the word וַיְהִי is a reversing *vav*, a grammatical concept that will be introduced as one of the Building Blocks of the next chapter. It is not simply the prefix meaning "and." That is why the phrase וַיְהִי עֶרֶב does not simply mean the same thing as יְהִי עֶרֶב with the word "and" added.

Exercises

Exercise 2 [page 7]

2. Draw a line connecting each Hebrew word to its English translation. For some words, there can be more than one correct translation.

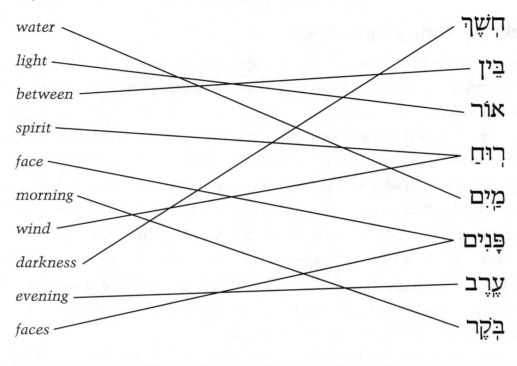

water
light
between
spirit
face
morning
wind
darkness
evening
faces

חֹשֶׁךְ
בֵּין
אוֹר
רוּחַ
מַיִם
פָּנִים
עֶרֶב
בֹּקֶר

Exercise 3 [page 7]

3. The following are plural forms of nouns introduced as vocabulary in this chapter. Draw a line connecting each plural noun to its singular form. Translate both into English.

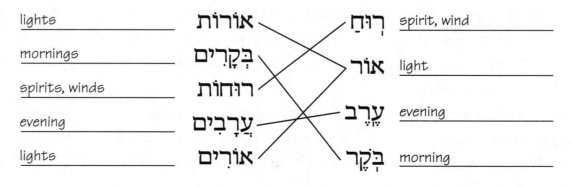

lights _____ אוֹרוֹת

mornings _____ בְּקָרִים

spirits, winds _____ רוּחוֹת

evening _____ עֲרָבִים

lights _____ אוֹרִים

רוּחַ spirit, wind _____

אוֹר light _____

עֶרֶב evening _____

בֹּקֶר morning _____

Exercise 4 [page 8]

a. good morning

good evening

good night

a good name (*Students may recognize this phrase from the name of the founder of Chasidism, the Baal Shem Tov, Master of the Good Name.*)

a good day (*This is also used in the prayer book to mean "festival" or "holiday." The Yiddish word for holiday,* yontif, *comes from this Hebrew.*)

b. a big/great wind/spirit

the spirit of God

spirit of life

the spirit of his holiness *or (more idiomatically)* his holy spirit

the winds/spirits of heaven/the sky

c. between/among you *(m sg)*

between/among you *(m pl)*

between/among us

between/among him/it

between/among the Children of Israel

d. the light of your *(m sg)* face

in/with/by the light of your *(m sg)* face (*This phrase appears in the second line of* Sim Shalom, *the blessing for peace, found in the gender-sensitive* Gates of Prayer *on page 122.*)

the face of the lord/ruler

the face of God

the face/surface of the earth/ground/land

e. the light of morning

a light to/for the nations (*a phrase derived from Isaiah 42:6 and 49:6, used to describe the task of Israel: to be a light unto the nations*)

darkness and light

a land of darkness

a day of darkness

f. bread and water

living water/waters (*Note: this is an adjective and noun combination, not the word pair "waters of life." A word-pair would use the word pair form of* מַיִם, *which is* מֵי*.)*

many/great/abundant water/waters

holy waters

water of/waters of Egypt

Exercise 5 [page 9]

Translation	Root	Participle
say, tell *m sg*	א־מ־ר	אוֹמֵר
bless *m sg*	ב־ר־ך	מְבָרֵךְ
praise *m sg*	ה־ל־ל	מְהַלֵּל
help *m sg*	ע־ז־ר	עוֹזֵר
say, tell *m pl*	א־מ־ר	אוֹמְרִים
speak *m pl*	ד־ב־ר	מְדַבְּרִים
reign, rule *m pl*	מ־ל־ך	מוֹלְכִים
create *m sg*	ב־ר־א	בּוֹרֵא
guard, keep *m pl*	ש־מ־ר	שׁוֹמְרִים
choose *m sg*	ב־ח־ר	בּוֹחֵר

Notes on

Torah Study Text: Vocabulary and Root Review [page 10]

This section can serve as a quick review of the material introduced in the first chapter of the unit: the new vocabulary and Hebrew roots. Since it can be intimidating for some students to reveal what they know, or don't know, in front of a group, it may be preferable for students to go over this section individually, or in *chevruta*, learning pairs, while the teacher circulates among them to assess how much they have been able to retain.

Some of the exercises from the previous chapter may also be used as a classroom review.

Building Blocks

Tenses in Hebrew [page 10]

The Building Blocks in each chapter contain the core grammatical concepts that students should understand before progressing to the next unit. This material is probably most effectively presented by the teacher to the entire group. Following are additional details that you may wish to include in your presentation.

In modern Hebrew, there are tenses: past, present, and future. In classical Hebrew, there are perfect verbs (which in modern Hebrew are used for the past tense), participles (which in modern Hebrew are used for the present tense), and imperfect verbs (which in modern Hebrew are used for the future tense). You may want to remind your students that in Chapter 4 of *Aleph Isn't Enough,* we introduced the participle, a verb form that can act as a noun or as a verb. In classical Hebrew, the participle can be translated into English as a present tense verb form and as continuing action in the past, present, or future.

Perfect Verbs [page 10]

The concept of different Hebrew verb patterns will be more fully explained in Chapter 8, Unit 4, when the (פָּעַל) pattern is introduced. Until that unit, all the Building Blocks will refer to the simple (פָּעַל) pattern.

The regular vowel pattern for simple (פָּעַל) perfect הוּא forms is ▪ ַ ▪ ָ. The variation

■ ▪ ▪ occurs whenever the final root letter is א or ה, such as in the verbs: קָרָא, הָיָה, and בָּרָא.

Imperfect Verbs [page 11]

There are two different regular vowel patterns for simple (פָּעַל) imperfect הוּא forms: ■ ▪ ▪יִ and ■ ▪ ▪יִ. However, many different variations in voweling exist, especially if the first or last root letter is ע, ח, ה, or א. This is the case with most of the verb roots introduced thus far, as illustrated in the Grammar Enrichment chart on page 13. For this reason, we have introduced only the prefix י without vowels as the indicator for imperfect הוּא forms.

Students may recognize the imperfect verb יַעֲשֶׂה from the prayer *Oseh Shalom*, found in the gender-sensitive *Gates of Prayer* on page 64. It is a good example of an imperfect verb used to indicate action wished or urged: "May [God] make peace."

The Reversing *Vav* [page 11]

It is generally not difficult to distinguish between a reversing *vav* and the prefix meaning "and." A reversing *vav* will only be attached to an imperfect or perfect verb. The subject will come after the verb. And whenever a reversing *vav* is attached to an imperfect verb, it will be voweled as either וַ or וָ. Whenever a reversing *vav* is attached to a perfect verb, it will include the same vowel as the prefix meaning "and," which is generally וְ or וּ.

Torah Study Text with Building Blocks [page 12]

Many of the words highlighted in this passage are imperfect or perfect forms of unfamiliar roots. Reassure your students that they are not expected to know all these roots. They are highlighted simply to illustrate the grammatical forms just introduced as Building Blocks.

There are only two perfect forms among the highlighted verbs: בָּרָא and קָרָא. As indicated above, both contain the irregular vowel pattern because of the final root letter א.

The verb וַיַּרְא (along with וַיְהִי) provides an example of the disappearance of the final root letter ה when the reversing *vav* is added. The root of וַיַּרְא is ר־א־ה.

Additional Reading and Translation Practice [pages 14–17]

You may wish to have your students work on this section in *chevruta*, learning pairs. Some or all of this material can also be left for homework.

1. עוֹשֶׂה שָׁלוֹם can be found in the gender-sensitive *Gates of Prayer* on page 64. You may wish to point out to your students that the new root א־מ־ר appears in this

excerpt in the word אִמְרוּ, a plural command meaning "[All of you] Say: Amen!"

2. אֲדוֹן עוֹלָם can be found in the gray gender-sensitive *Gates of Prayer* on page 156. This excerpt contains the participle הֹוֶה in the phrase

וְהוּא הָיָה וְהוּא הֹוֶה וְהוּא יִהְיֶה. There are differing interpretations of the root of this participle. Some sources take the view, as we have in our text, that there is no participle form of the root ה-י-ה and regard the participle הֹוֶה as a form of the root ה-ו-ה. Others regard הֹוֶה as a participle form of the root ה-י-ה.

3. The passage from the Torah Service (from Psalm 10:16, Psalm 93:1 and Exodus 15:18) can be found in the gender-sensitive *Gates of Prayer* on page 142.

4. וְנֶאֱמַר (Zechariah 14:9) can be found in the gender-sensitive *Gates of Prayer* on page 149.

5. The blessings for sons (from Genesis 48:20) and daughters can be found in *On the Doorposts of Your House: Prayers and Ceremonies for the Jewish Home* on pages 39 and 40.

Exercises

Exercise 1 [page 18]

Form	Root	Verb	Form	Root	Verb
perfect	י-צ-א	יָצָא	participle	נ-ת-ן	נוֹתֵן
imperfect	ז-כ-ר	יִזְכֹּר	perfect	ה-י-ה	הָיָה
imperfect	א-מ-ר	יֹאמַר	perfect	א-ה-ב	אָהַב
participle	א-מ-ר	אוֹמֵר	imperfect	ע-ש-ה	יַעֲשֶׂה
imperfect	ע-ז-ר	יַעֲזֹר	imperfect	א-כ-ל	יֹאכַל
participle	ב-ח-ר	בּוֹחֵר	imperfect	ה-י-ה	יִהְיֶה
perfect	ר-פ-א	רָפָא	perfect	ע-ז-ר	עָזַר
perfect	מ-ל-ך	מָלַךְ	participle	ש-מ-ר	שׁוֹמֵר

Notes on

Torah Study Text: Genesis 4:1–5, 8–10 [page 22]

Following are all the words, roots, endings, and prefixes appearing in Genesis 4:1–5, 8–10 that have already been introduced. The book and chapter in which they were introduced is indicated in parentheses.

Genesis 4:1–5

¹וְהָאָדָם יָדַע אֶת־חַוָּה אִשְׁתּוֹ וַתַּהַר וַתֵּלֶד אֶת־קַיִן וַתֹּאמֶר קָנִיתִי אִישׁ אֶת־יְהֹוָה: ²וַתֹּסֶף לָלֶדֶת אֶת־אָחִיו אֶת־הָבֶל וַיְהִי־הֶבֶל רֹעֵה צֹאן וְקַיִן הָיָה עֹבֵד אֲדָמָה: ³וַיְהִי מִקֵּץ יָמִים וַיָּבֵא קַיִן מִפְּרִי הָאֲדָמָה מִנְחָה לַיהֹוָה: ⁴וְהֶבֶל הֵבִיא גַם־הוּא מִבְּכֹרוֹת צֹאנוֹ וּמֵחֶלְבֵהֶן וַיִּשַׁע יְהֹוָה אֶל־הֶבֶל וְאֶל־מִנְחָתוֹ: ⁵וְאֶל־קַיִן וְאֶל־מִנְחָתוֹ לֹא שָׁעָה וַיִּחַר לְקַיִן מְאֹד וַיִּפְּלוּ פָּנָיו:

Genesis 4:8–10

⁸וַיֹּאמֶר קַיִן אֶל־הֶבֶל אָחִיו וַיְהִי בִּהְיוֹתָם בַּשָּׂדֶה וַיָּקָם קַיִן אֶל־הֶבֶל אָחִיו וַיַּהַרְגֵהוּ: ⁹וַיֹּאמֶר יְהֹוָה אֶל־קַיִן אֵי הֶבֶל אָחִיךָ וַיֹּאמֶר לֹא יָדַעְתִּי הֲשֹׁמֵר אָחִי אָנֹכִי: ¹⁰וַיֹּאמֶר מֶה עָשִׂיתָ קוֹל דְּמֵי אָחִיךָ צֹעֲקִים אֵלַי מִן־הָאֲדָמָה:

the *(attached prefix) (A.I.E. Ch 1), appears on the following words:*

הַ, הָ — וְהָאָדָם, הָאֲדָמָה

the word הֲשֹׁמֵר *in verse 9 does not mean* **the** *but is the question indicator, as will be explained in the Building Blocks of this unit, Chapter 4*

and *(attached prefix) (A.I.E. Ch 2), appears on the following words:*

וְ, וָ, וּ — וְהָאָדָם, וְקַיִן, וְהֶבֶל, וּמֵחֶלְבֵהֶן, וְאֶל

the vav on the following words is a reversing vav, though it may also be translated as **and:**

וַתַּהַר, וַתֵּלֶד, וַתֹּאמֶר, וַתֹּסֶף, וַיְהִי, וַיָּבֵא, וַיֹּשַׁע, וַיִּחַר,
וַיִּפְּלוּ, וַיֹּאמֶר, וַיָּקָם, וַיַּהַרְגֵהוּ

definite direct object marker (untranslatable) (A.I.E. Ch 4), appears four times —	אֵת, אֶת

in our Torah Study Text; appears one additional time as the preposition with as explained in this chapter on page 36

his (attached ending) m sg (A.I.E. Ch 9), appears on the following words: —	־וֹ, יו

אִשְׁתּוֹ, אָחִיו, צֹאנוֹ, מִנְחָתוֹ, פָּנָיו

say, utter, tell (B.I.F.B. Ch 1), appears in the following words: וַתֹּאמֶר, וַיֹּאמֶר —	א־מ־ר
to, for (attached preposition) (A.I.E. Ch 8) —	לְ־

(with the vowels לַ or לֵ it generally means to the, for the, though not with an infinitive such as לָלֶדֶת, to give birth, to bear); appears on the following words: לָלֶדֶת, לַיהוָֹה, לְקַיִן

be, exist (B.I.F.B. Ch 1), appears in the following words: וַיְהִי, הָיָה, בִּהְיוֹתָם —	ה־י־ה
earth, ground, land f (A.I.E. Ch 8) —	אֲדָמָה
plural of יוֹם, day m (A.I.E. Ch 3) —	יָמִים
from, than (attached preposition) (A.I.E. Ch 10), appears on the following words: מִפְּרִי, מִבְּכֹרוֹת, וּמֵחֶלְבֵהֶן —	מִ־, מֵי־
(A.I.E. Ch 3) fruit m —	פְּרִי
he, it m (A.I.E. Ch 1) —	הוּא
פָּנִים with attached ending, face m pl and f pl (B.I.F.B. Ch 1) —	פָּנָיו
with, in (attached preposition) (A.I.E. Ch 6), appears on the following words: בִּהְיוֹתָם, בַּשָּׂדֶה —	בְּ־
their, them (attached ending) (B.I.F.B. Ch 5), appears on the word בִּהְיוֹתָם —	־ָם
him, it (attached ending) m sg (A.I.E. Ch 9), appears on the word וַיַּהַרְגֵהוּ —	־הוּ
your, you (attached ending) m sg (A.I.E. Ch 6), appears on the word אָחִיךָ —	־ךָ

guard, keep, preserve *(A.I.E. Ch 3), appears in the word* הִשָּׁמֶר	—	שׁ־מ־ר
make, do, act *(A.I.E. Ch 7), appears on the word* עָשִׂיתָ	—	ע־שׂ־ה
from, than *(A.I.E. Ch 10)*	—	מִן

Translating the Torah Study Text [pages 23–25]

As your students work on their translations, the following comments may assist them:

1. You may wish to refer them to page 36 in this chapter, to explain about the preposition אֵת. Otherwise, they may be confused by its translation as "with" in verse 1.

2. When a verb has a reversing *vav* attached, there may not be a subject indicated, other than the subject implied by the gender or form of the verb, such as in verse 1: וַתַּהַר וַתֵּלֶד, "and she conceived and she bore." If there is a subject indicated for a verb with a reversing *vav*, the subject will always come after the verb. Examples: וַיְהִי הֶבֶל, "Hevel [Abel] became/was" (verse 2); וַיָּבֵא קַיִן, "Kayin [Cain] brought" (verse 3).

3. A participle can act as a noun and join with another noun in a word pair, as in עֹבֵד אֲדָמָה, "a worker of the earth/ground," in verse 2.

4. The words in a word pair can have prefixes or endings attached, as in מִפְּרִי הָאֲדָמָה, "**from** the fruit of the earth/ground," in verse 3. Remember, too, that if the last word of the word pair is definite, as in מִפְּרִי הָאֲדָמָה, both words in the word pair can be translated as definite:, "from **the** fruit of **the** earth." A word is definite not only if the prefix ה is attached, but also if it has a pronoun ending, as in צֹאנוֹ, "**his** flock" (verse 4): מִבְּכֹרוֹת צֹאנוֹ, "from **the** firstborn of **his** flock."

[pages 25–27]

Older translations of the Bible, including our fourth translation cited, the *Jerusalem Bible*, tended to translate every *vav* as "and": "*And* the man knew his wife…*and* she conceived *and* she bore…*and* Abel was a shepherd…." More recent translations reflect the idea (presented as a Building Block in this chapter on pages 29–30) that the reversing *vav* is a narrative device indicating sequential action and therefore can be translated as "then" or "now" or "so" or even left untranslated.

Similarly, the nonreversing *vav*, generally meaning the conjunction "and," sometimes indicates a disjunction: "but." An example of this is found in verse 5: וְאֶל קַיִן; three of our four translations render it as "**but** to Cain/Qayin," while Everett Fox leaves it untranslated.

You may wish to comment on the differing orientations of our four translations as illustrated by their treatment of the four-letter name of God. Both the Jewish Publication Society translation from 1999 and the *Jerusalem Bible* translation from 1969 reflect the Jewish practice of pronouncing the word *Adonai* in place of the unpronounceable four-letter name of God. *Adonai* is a form of the Hebrew אָדוֹן, meaning "lord"; these two translations use "the Lord" in the English wherever the four-letter Divine Name appears in the Hebrew.

The more traditional orientation of the ArtScroll *Chumash* is reflected in its translation of the Divine Name as "Hashem," meaning "the Name." Among more traditional Jews, the word *Adonai* is only used when engaged in prayer; otherwise, *Hashem* is used when speaking of God.

Everett Fox follows the scholarly practice of rendering the name of God by the English equivalents of the four Hebrew letters: "Yhwh." (The "W" is used instead of a "V" for the *vav* because that is how the letter was pronounced in antiquity.) This approach avoids assigning a meaning or pronunciation to the Divine Name, reflecting the way it appears in the Hebrew.

Vocabulary [page 28]

All the new vocabulary words are identified and highlighted within the Torah Study Text at the beginning of Chapter 4, on page 36.

1. The word אִשָּׁה, "woman/wife," appears only with the וֹ pronoun ending, meaning "his": אִשְׁתּוֹ, "his wife."

2. The word אָח, "brother," appears only with pronoun endings: אָחִיו, "his brother"; אָחִיךָ, "your brother", and אָחִי, "my brother."

3. The word דָּם appears only in a plural word-pair form: דְּמֵי אָחִיךָ, "the blood(s) of your brother."

The Hebrew Root [pages 28–30]

Some verb forms of the root יָ־דַ־ע contain variations, caused by both the first root letter י and the last root letter ע:

1. For verbs with the final root letter ע, such as יָ־דַ־ע and שָׁ־מַ־ע, the simple (פָּעַל) participle form is *(masculine singular)* עַ◻וֹ◻ and ◻וֹ◻ת *(feminine singular)*. The plural participle forms are regular.

2. For verbs with first root letter י, such as יָ־דַ־ע and יָ־צָ־א, the י drops out in the imperfect forms.

You may want to remind your students that participle, perfect, and imperfect forms of all roots introduced in this book (and in *Aleph Isn't Enough*) are included in the verb charts in the back of their books.

Building Blocks

More on the Reversing *Vav* [pages 30–31]

The verbs used in this example are all imperfect feminine forms; hence they begin with the letter תּ. This form will be taught in the Building Blocks section of Chapter 4.

Torah Commentary [pages 31–32]

The passage from the Talmud, Tractate *Sanhedrin*, is included here because so many people are familiar with the quote, often used in Jewish fund-raising and social action appeals, that "one who saves a single life is regarded as having saved an entire world." Here the larger context of that quote is provided, derived from the commentary on the plural form of דָּם appearing in verse 10.

Exercises

Exercise 2 [page 33]

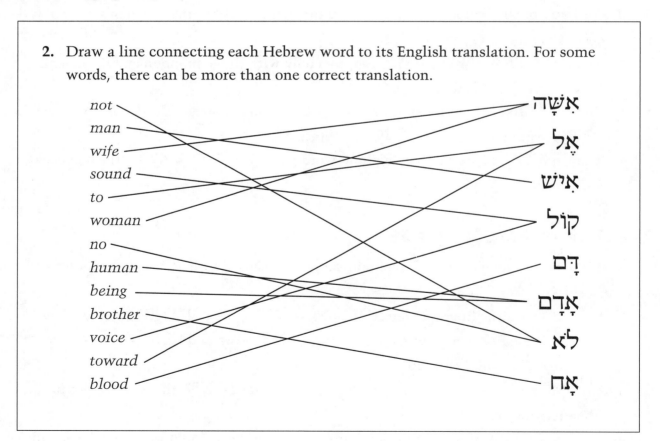

2. Draw a line connecting each Hebrew word to its English translation. For some words, there can be more than one correct translation.

not	אִשָּׁה
man	אֶל
wife	אִישׁ
sound	קוֹל
to	דָּם
woman	אָדָם
no	לֹא
human	אָח
being	
brother	
voice	
toward	
blood	

Exercise 3 [page 33]

3. The following are plural forms of nouns introduced as vocabulary in this chapter. Both אִישׁ and אִשָּׁה have irregular plural forms, listed here and in the Glossary. Draw a line connecting each plural noun to its singular form. Translate both into English.

women, wives _____	נָשִׁים אִישׁ	man _____
brothers _____	אָחִים דָּם	blood _____
men _____	אֲנָשִׁים אִשָּׁה	woman, wife _____
blood(s) _____	דָּמִים קוֹל	sound, voice _____
sounds, voices _____	קוֹלוֹת אָח	brother _____

Exercise 4 [page 34]

a. soul/breath of man/humankind/a human being

   words of man/humankind/a human being

   the blood of humankind/a human being

   hand of man/humankind/a human being

   [the] acts/works/deeds of [the] hands of man/humankind/a human being

b. sound of water

   the voice/sound of the people/nation

   sound of the shofar

   sound/voice of humankind/man/a human being

   spirit of humankind/man/a human being

c. every man

   a mighty man

   a man of kindness

   people of truth *(many synagogues bear this name)*

   men and women

d. a big brother

   the voice of your brother

a man to his brother

a covenant of brothers

peace of your brothers

e. heart of a woman, a woman's heart

way of a woman, a woman's way

your (m sg) woman/wife

the wife of his son

the wives of the king

f. blood of men/people

blood of slaves/servants

blood of the face

face to face

not to/toward the house

Exercise 5 [pages 34–35]

Translation	Root	Participle
sanctify m sg	ק־ד־שׁ	מְקַדֵּשׁ
work, serve m sg	ע־ב־ד	עוֹבֵד
give m pl	נ־ת־ן	נוֹתְנִים
know m pl	י־ד־ע	יוֹדְעִים
command m sg	צ־ו־ה	מְצַוֶּה
know m sg	י־ד־ע	יוֹדֵעַ
say, tell f sg	א־מ־ר	אוֹמֶרֶת
work, serve f pl	ע־ב־ד	עוֹבְדוֹת
hear m sg	שׁ־מ־ע	שׁוֹמֵעַ
eat m pl	א־כ־ל	אוֹכְלִים

Notes on

Torah Study Text: Vocabulary and Root Review [page 36]

It is sufficient for students to recall the meaning of the root for highlighted verb forms. For example, while students were introduced in Chapter 3 to the root יָ־דַ־ע, meaning "know," they have not yet been introduced to the perfect אֲנִי form יָדַעְתִּי: "I knew." Vocabulary words that appear in our Torah Study Text in variant forms or with prefixes or suffixes attached were noted in the Vocabulary section of the previous chapter of this Teacher's Guide.

Building Blocks:

The Question ה [page 38]

Some students may think that the ה on the word pair הֲשֹׁמֵר אָחִי means "the": "**the** guard/keeper of my brother." Remind your students that the definite article ה (meaning "the") is never added to the first word of a word pair. Only the last word of a word pair can be definite, and when it is, then the entire word pair is definite. שֹׁמֵר אָחִי, without the ה, already means "**the** guard/keeper of my brother" because the last word of the word pair אָחִי, "my brother," is definite.

Torah Study Text with Building Blocks [page 38]

Many of the words highlighted in this passage are imperfect forms of unfamiliar roots. Reassure your students that they are not expected to know all these roots. They are highlighted simply to illustrate the grammatical forms just introduced as Building Blocks.

[page 39]

This chart includes feminine forms of the root בָּ־רָ־א, despite the fact that such forms would never appear in the *Tanach* or anywhere in classical literature. (As explained in Chapter 3 of *Aleph Isn't Enough*, the root בָּ־רָ־א signifies divine, as opposed to human, creation, and God is virtually always grammatically masculine in classical Hebrew texts.) Feminine forms of the root בָּ־רָ־א are, however, used in some contemporary feminist liturgy (e.g., בּוֹרֵאת פְּרִי הַגֶּפֶן) and for that reason these forms are included in this chart.

While students are not expected to memorize the information in this chart, it is certainly helpful for them to begin to notice patterns and variations. The feminine perfect form הָיְתָה appeared in the Torah Study Text of the first unit, Genesis 1:2: וְהָאָרֶץ הָיְתָה תֹהוּ וָבֹהוּ, "And the earth/land **was** nothingness and void." The feminine imperfect form תֵּצֵא may be familiar to some students from the passage in the Torah service from Isaiah 2:3, found on page 142 in the gender-sensitive *Gates of Prayer*: כִּי מִצִּיּוֹן תֵּצֵא תוֹרָה, "for from Zion will go out Torah."

Additional Reading and Translation Practice [pages 40–43]

1. Psalm 150:6: This line can be found in the morning service in *Gates of Prayer: The New Union Prayerbook* on page 297.

2. נִשְׁמַת כָּל חַי can be found in *Gates of Prayer: The New Union Prayerbook* on page 297.

3. הַתִּקְוָה can be found in *Gates of Prayer: The New Union Prayerbook* on page 765.

Exercises

Exercise 1 [page 43]

Form	Root	Masculine	Feminine
participle	י־ד־ע	יוֹדֵעַ	יָדְעָה
perfect	א־מ־ר	אָמַר	עָבְדָה
imperfect	ע־ב־ד	יַעֲבֹד	תִּהְיֶה
participle	ב־ר־א	בּוֹרֵא	יוֹדַעַת
perfect	י־ד־ע	יָדַע	תֹּאמַר
imperfect	א־כ־ל	יֹאכַל	בּוֹרֵאת
participle	ע־ב־ד	עוֹבֵד	בָּחֲרָה
imperfect	ה־י־ה	יִהְיֶה	תַּעֲבֹד
perfect	ע־ב־ד	עָבַד	עוֹבֶדֶת
imperfect	א־מ־ר	יֹאמַר	אָמְרָה
perfect	ב־ח־ר	בָּחַר	תֹּאכַל

Notes on

Torah Study Text: Genesis 11:1–9 [page 48]

Following are all the words, roots, endings, and prefixes appearing in Genesis 11:1–9 that have already been introduced. The book and chapter in which they were introduced is indicated in parentheses.

¹וַיְהִי כָל־הָאָרֶץ שָׂפָה אֶחָת וּדְבָרִים אֲחָדִים: ²וַיְהִי בְּנָסְעָם מִקֶּדֶם וַיִּמְצְאוּ בִקְעָה בְּאֶרֶץ שִׁנְעָר וַיֵּשְׁבוּ שָׁם: ³וַיֹּאמְרוּ אִישׁ אֶל־רֵעֵהוּ הָבָה נִלְבְּנָה לְבֵנִים וְנִשְׂרְפָה לִשְׂרֵפָה וַתְּהִי לָהֶם הַלְּבֵנָה לְאָבֶן וְהַחֵמָר הָיָה לָהֶם לַחֹמֶר: ⁴וַיֹּאמְרוּ הָבָה נִבְנֶה־לָּנוּ עִיר וּמִגְדָּל וְרֹאשׁוֹ בַשָּׁמַיִם וְנַעֲשֶׂה־לָּנוּ שֵׁם פֶּן־נָפוּץ עַל־פְּנֵי כָל־הָאָרֶץ: ⁵וַיֵּרֶד יְהֹוָה לִרְאֹת אֶת־הָעִיר וְאֶת־הַמִּגְדָּל אֲשֶׁר בָּנוּ בְּנֵי הָאָדָם: ⁶וַיֹּאמֶר יְהֹוָה הֵן עַם אֶחָד וְשָׂפָה אַחַת לְכֻלָּם וְזֶה הַחִלָּם לַעֲשׂוֹת וְעַתָּה לֹא־יִבָּצֵר מֵהֶם כֹּל אֲשֶׁר יָזְמוּ לַעֲשׂוֹת: ⁷הָבָה נֵרְדָה וְנָבְלָה שָׁם שְׂפָתָם אֲשֶׁר לֹא יִשְׁמְעוּ אִישׁ שְׂפַת רֵעֵהוּ: ⁸וַיָּפֶץ יְהֹוָה אֹתָם מִשָּׁם עַל־פְּנֵי כָל־הָאָרֶץ וַיַּחְדְּלוּ לִבְנֹת הָעִיר: ⁹עַל־כֵּן קָרָא שְׁמָהּ בָּבֶל כִּי־שָׁם בָּלַל יְהֹוָה שְׂפַת כָּל־הָאָרֶץ וּמִשָּׁם הֱפִיצָם יְהֹוָה עַל־פְּנֵי כָּל־הָאָרֶץ:

be, exist *(B.I.F.B. Ch 1)*, appears in the following words:

ה־י־ה   —   וַיְהִי, הָיָה, וַתְּהִי

and *(attached prefix) (A.I.E. Ch 2)*, appears on the following words:

וְ־, וּ־   —

וּדְבָרִים, וְנִשְׂרְפָה, וְהַחֵמָר, וּמִגְדָּל, וְרֹאשׁוֹ, וְנַעֲשֶׂה, וְאֶת, וְשָׂפָה, וְזֶה, וְעַתָּה, וּמִשָּׁם

the vav on the following words is a reversing vav, **though it may also be translated as and:**

וַיְהִי, וַיִּמְצְאוּ, וַיֵּשְׁבוּ, וַיֹּאמְרוּ, וַתְּהִי, וַיֵּרֶד, וַיֹּאמֶר, וַיָּפֶץ, וַיַּחְדְּלוּ

all, every *(A.I.E. Ch 8)* —	כֹּל, כָּל, כָּל
earth, land *f (A.I.E. Ch 3)* —	אֶרֶץ

(אֶרֶץ *becomes* אָרֶץ *when the prefix* הָ, *the, is attached*)

the *(attached prefix) (A.I.E. Ch 1)*, appears on the following words: —	הַ־, הָ־

הָאָרֶץ, הַלְּבֵנָה, הָעִיר, הַמִּגְדָּל, הָאָדָם

word, speech *(A.I.E. Ch 10) m* —	דָּבָר
plural ending *(A.I.E. Ch 2)*, appears on the following words:	־ִים

וּדְבָרִים, אֲחָדִים, לְבֵנִים —

with, in *(attached preposition) (A.I.E. Ch 6)*, appears on the following words: —	בְּ־, בַ־

בְּנָסְעָם, בִקְעָה, בְּאֶרֶץ, בַּשָּׁמַיִם, בָּנוּ

their, them *(attached ending) (B.I.F.B. Ch 5)*, appears on the following words: —	־ָם

בְּנָסְעָם, לְכֻלָּם, שְׂפָתָם, אֹתָם, הֲפִיצָם

from, than *(attached preposition) (A.I.E. Ch 10)*, appears on the following words: —	מִ־, מֵי־

מִקֶּדֶם, מֵהֶם, מִשָּׁם, וּמִשָּׁם

say, utter, tell *(B.I.F.B. Ch 1)* appears in the following words: וַיֹּאמְרוּ, וַיֹּאמֶר —	א־מ־ר
him, it *(attached ending) m sg (A.I.E. Ch 9)*, appears on the word רֵעֵהוּ —	־הוּ
to, for *(attached preposition) (A.I.E. Ch 8)* appears on the following words: —	לְ־

לִשְׂרֵפָה, לָהֶם, לְאָבֶן, לַחֹמֶר, לָנוּ, לִרְאֹת, לְכֻלָּם, לַעֲשׂוֹת, לִבְנֹת

our, us *(attached ending) (A.I.E. Ch 7)* appears on the word לָנוּ —	־נוּ
his *(attached ending) m sg (A.I.E. Ch 9)*, appears on the word וְרֹאשׁוֹ —	־וֹ
heavens, sky *m (A.I.E. Ch 3)* —	שָׁמַיִם
make, do, act *(A.I.E. Ch 7)*, appears in the following words: וְנַעֲשֶׂה, לַעֲשׂוֹת —	ע־שׂ־ה
name *m (A.I.E. Ch 1)* —	שֵׁם
on, about *(A.I.E. Ch 8)* —	עַל

word-pair form of פָּנִים, face, surface *m pl* and *f pl* (*B.I.F.B. Ch 1*)	—	פְּנֵי
definite direct object marker (untranslatable) (*A.I.E. Ch 4*), appears two times in our Torah Study Text and once with a pronoun ending: אֹתָם	—	אֶת, אֵת
who, that, which (*A.I.E. Ch 8*)	—	אֲשֶׁר
plural word-pair form of בֵּן, son, child *m* (*A.I.E. Ch 3*)	—	בְּנֵי
human being, man, humankind *m* (*B.I.F.B. Ch 3*)	—	אָדָם
people, nation *m* (*A.I.E. Ch 4*)	—	עַם
no, not (*B.I.F.B. Ch 3*)	—	לֹא
hear, listen, obey (*A.I.E. Ch 1*), appears in the word יִשְׁמְעוּ	—	שׁ־מ־ע
(*B.I.F.B. Ch 3*) man *m*	—	אִישׁ
her, its, it (attached ending) *f sg* (*A.I.E. Ch 9*), appears on the word שְׁמָה	—	◌ָהּ

Translating the Torah Study Text [pages 49–50]

As your students work on their translations, the following comments may assist them:

1. The word וַיְהִי, "and [it] was," can have a subject, as in verse 1: וַיְהִי כָל־הָאָרֶץ, "and all the earth was." It can also appear without a subject, as in the beginning of verse 2. In such cases, it is often understood to mean "it happened" or "it came to pass" (which is how it is treated by two of our translations cited).

2. Remind your students that there is no word for "a" or "an" in Hebrew. They must insert it in their translations as needed, for example, (verse 4). וַיִּמְצְאוּ בִקְעָה, "they found **a** valley," (verse 2) נִבְנֶה לָּנוּ עִיר, "let us build for us **a** city"

3. As indicated in the notes to the new vocabulary introduced in this chapter, the word רֵעַ has a range of meanings. It is this word that appears in the famous passage in Leviticus 19:18, וְאָהַבְתָּ לְרֵעֲךָ כָּמוֹךָ, "you shall love your neighbor as yourself." It is also used idiomatically with the word אִישׁ, "man," as in verses 3 and 7, to mean אִישׁ...רֵעֵהוּ, "one...another" (and is translated in this way in three of our four translations).

4. When translating verbs that have been made negative by the placement of לֹא, "no/not," before them, one must adjust the word order a bit in the English translation,

such as in verse 7, אֲשֶׁר לֹא יִשְׁמְעוּ אִישׁ שְׂפַת רֵעֵהוּ, which would not sound appropriate if left in its Hebrew word order: "that not they understand a man the language of his neighbor." but must be reordered to read "that a man not understand the language of his neighbor" or "that they not understand one another."

[pages 51–53]

Sometimes variations in translation occur because there is an awkward or usual phrase in the Hebrew. Verse 3, for example, contains the wording הָבָה נִלְבְּנָה לְבֵנִים וְנִשְׂרְפָה לִשְׂרֵפָה, "come let us make bricks and let us burn to burning." What do those last two words, which we have literally translated "and let us burn to burning," really mean? Each of our translations renders them slightly differently: "and burn them hard," "and burn them in fire," "and let us burn them well-burnt," or "and burn them thoroughly."

Sometimes variations in translation reflect differences in interpretation. As noted previously, every translation is an interpretation, and in some instances this is more apparent than others. Notice, for example, in verse 1, that three of our translations render the phrase דְּבָרִים אֲחָדִים as having to do with language: "the same words," "one set-of-words," or "of one speech." The ArtScroll *Chumash* goes one step beyond this literal meaning in its translation, offering an interpretation of what those words might imply: "of common purpose."

Another example is provided in verse 6, where the Hebrew states, כֹּל אֲשֶׁר יָזְמוּ לַעֲשׂוֹת וְעַתָּה לֹא־יִבָּצֵר מֵהֶם. Three of our translations understand this to be a statement: "then nothing that they may propose to do will be out of their reach," or "now there will be no barrier for them in all that they scheme to do!" or "and now nothing will be withheld from them, which they have schemed to do." The ArtScroll *Chumash* is the only one that renders this as a question: "And now, should it not be withheld from them all they propose to do?" The Hebrew could be understood in either way, as a question or as a statement, but the way that God appears (threatened? anxious? or powerful? in control?) is quite different with each translation.

Vocabulary [page 54]

All the new vocabulary words are identified and highlighted within the Torah Study Text at the beginning of Chapter 6, on page 61.

1. The word אֶחָד, "one," will be familiar to many students from the *Shema* (in the gender-sensitive *Gates of Prayer* on page 51). It appears in verse 1 as a masculine plural adjective with the meaning "some/a few."

2. The word אַחַת, "one," may be familiar to some students from the third of the Four Questions of the Passover seder:

שֶׁבְּכָל הַלֵּילוֹת אֵין אָנוּ מַטְבִּילִין אֲפִילוּ פַּעַם אֶחָת. (The Passover Four Questions can be found in the CCAR Haggadah *The Open Door* on page 30.)

3. The word רֵעַ appears in the Torah Study Text twice, both times with the pronoun ending: רֵעֵהוּ.

4. The word רֹאשׁ, "head/top/beginning," will be familiar to many students from the holiday רֹאשׁ הַשָּׁנָה, the Jewish New Year (literally: "the head/beginning of the year"). It appears only once in our Torah Study Text, with a pronoun ending and prefix *vav* meaning "and": וְרֹאשׁוֹ, "and its head/top."

5. The word שָׁם may be familiar to some students because the four letters on the Chanukah dreidel נ, ג, ה, שׁ are said to represent a Hebrew sentence: נֵס גָּדוֹל הָיָה שָׁם, "a great miracle happened **there**."

The Hebrew Root: י־שׁ־ב [pages 54–55]

In verbs with the first root letter י, the י drops out in imperfect forms. We have already seen this with the roots י־ד־ע and י־צ־א. For the root י־שׁ־ב, the imperfect הוּא, "he," form is יֵשֵׁב, and the הִיא, "she," form is תֵּשֵׁב. These forms are included in the verb charts in the back of the book.

You may wish to mention to students that the word יִשּׁוּב, "population/settlement," appearing in the list of words derived from the root י־שׁ־ב, was the term for the Jewish population in Palestine during the period prior to the establishment of the State of Israel.

The Hebrew Root: ב־נ־ה [pages 55–56]

For verbs with the final root letter ה, such as the new root ב־נ־ה or the previously introduced root ע־שׂ־ה, the simple (פָּעַל) participle form is as shown in the text. The final root letter ה drops out in the plural forms, and the feminine singular form follows the pattern ה▢וֹ▢ instead of the usual pattern of ▢וֹ▢ֶת.

Torah Commentary [pages 56–57]

All of the commentaries in this chapter are from the medieval commentator Rashi, because he is the subject of this chapter's Extra Credit selection. You may wish to refer to the information provided about Rashi there before you go over his Torah commentaries.

Exercises

Exercise 2 [page 58]

2. Draw a line connecting each Hebrew word to its English translation. For some words, there can be more than one correct translation.

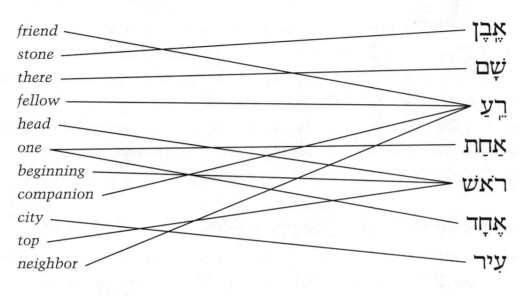

friend
stone
there
fellow
head
one
beginning
companion
city
top
neighbor

אֶבֶן
שָׁם
רֵעַ
אַחַת
רֹאשׁ
אֶחָד
עִיר

Exercise 3 [page 58]

3. The following are plural forms of words introduced as vocabulary in this chapter. Draw a line connecting each plural word to its singular form. Translate both into English.

cities _____

heads/tops/beginnings _____

some/a few _____

stones _____

some/a few _____

friends/neighbors/fellow
human beings/companions _____

עָרִים
רָאשִׁים
אֲחָדִים
אֲבָנִים
אֲחָדוֹת
רֵעִים

רֵעַ
אֶבֶן
אַחַת
עִיר
רֹאשׁ
אֶחָד

friend/neighbor/fellow/
human being/companion _____

stone _____

one _____

city _____

head/top/beginning _____

one _____

Exercise 4 [page 59]

a. one man

   one woman/wife

   one spirit

   one day

   a few days/some days

b. a good friend/neighbor/companion

   a brother and a friend

   the wife of his neighbor

   the blood of your neighbor/fellow human being

   the face of your neighbor/friend/companion/fellow human being

c. a big stone

   big stones

   some stones/a few stones

   a heart of stone

   the stones of Jerusalem

d. the head of the men/people

   the head of the Children of Israel

   the head of the nations/peoples

   the head of his friend/neighbor/companion, his friend's head

   the heads of the mighty ones

e. the city of the prophet

   the city of righteousness

   the city of holiness (*i.e., the Holy City—a name for Jerusalem*)

   the workers of the city

   the inhabitants (settlers/dwellers) of the cities

f. there

   there are the women

   the water that is there

   from there

   the light from there

Exercise 5 [pages 59–60]

Translation	Root	Participle
build *m pl*	ב־נ־ה	בּוֹנִים
make, do *m pl*	ע־שׂ־ה	עוֹשִׂים
work, serve *m sg*	ע־ב־ד	עוֹבֵד
sit, settle, dwell *m pl*	י־שׁ־ב	יוֹשְׁבִים
bring to life *m sg*	ח־י־ה	מְחַיֶּה
love *f sg*	א־ה־ב	אוֹהֶבֶת
sit, settle, dwell *m sg*	י־שׁ־ב	יוֹשֵׁב
remember *f pl*	ז־כ־ר	זוֹכְרוֹת
say, tell *m pl*	א־מ־ר	אוֹמְרִים
go out *m sg*	י־צ־א	יוֹצֵא
build *m sg*	ב־נ־ה	בּוֹנֶה
know *m sg*	י־ד־ע	יוֹדֵעַ

Notes on

Torah Study Text: Vocabulary and Root Review [page 61]

Only the vocabulary word or root itself is highlighted here, not any prefixes or suffixes that may be attached. Both new roots י־שׁ־ב and ב־נ־ה lose a root letter in their conjugated forms, leaving only two letters highlighted in most of the words in which they appear.

It is sufficient for students to recall the meaning of the root for highlighted verb forms. Students were introduced in Chapter 5 to the root י־שׁ־ב, meaning "sit/settle/dwell," but not to the plural imperfect form with reversing *vav*, וַיֵּשְׁבוּ, "and they settled/dwelt." Likewise, they should recall that the meaning of the root ב־נ־ה is "build," but they have not yet been introduced to any of the forms in which it appears in our Torah Study Text. The following information is provided solely for the teacher's assistance, in case students ask about these highlighted forms:

1. נִבְנֶה—an imperfect "we" form: "let us build" (The נ prefix is introduced in Chapter 10 of *Tav Is for Torah*.)

2. בָּנוּ—a perfect "they" form: "they built" (The plural perfect וּ ending will be introduced in this chapter. The final root letter ה drops out in plural perfect forms.)

3. לִבְנֹת—the infinitive: "to build."

Vocabulary words that appear in our Torah Study Text in variant forms or with prefixes or suffixes attached were noted in the Vocabulary section of the previous chapter of this Teacher's Guide.

Building Blocks

Plural Perfect and Imperfect Verbs [pages 62–63]

It is the regular form of plural perfect and imperfect verbs that is provided in the text. However, several of the roots introduced thus far have irregular forms. When introducing this material, it may be helpful to point out to students the irregularities that are noted in the Grammar Enrichment chart on page 65. It is helpful for students to be aware of certain "regular" irregularities, always caused by certain letters in certain positions within the root.

The Endings ◌ָם and הֶם [page 63]

The ◌ָם and הֶם endings are not used interchangeably. For example, as noted in the text, the ◌ָם ending is used with singular nouns, and the הֶם ending is used with plural nouns. Similarly, only the ◌ָם ending is used with certain prepositions, while only the הֶם ending is used with others.

Torah Study Text with Building Blocks [pages 63–64]

The new root בּ-נ-ה appears here in a plural perfect form: בָּנוּ. For roots with the final letter ה, the final ה drops out in the plural perfect form.

Additional Reading and Translation Practice [pages 66–70]

1. וְשָׁמְרוּ can be found in the gender-sensitive *Gates of Prayer* on page 55.

2. אַשְׁרֵי can be found in the gender-sensitive *Gates of Prayer* on pages 125–127.

3. בִּרְכַּת הַמָּזוֹן can be found in *On the Doorposts of Your House* on pages 9–18. The section containing the blessing for Jerusalem is on page 14.

4. The excerpt from Psalm 118 can be found in the short form of *Hallel* included in the gender-sensitive *Gates of Prayer* on page 176.

5. יִשְׂמְחוּ can be found in the gender-sensitive *Gates of Prayer* on page 118.

6. The excerpt from Isaiah 2:3 that appears in the Torah service can be found in the gender-sensitive *Gates of Prayer* on page 142.

Exercises

Exercise 1 [page 71]

a. his/its head/top/beginning

   her/its head/top/beginning

   your *(m sg)* head

   their head

   their heads/tops/beginnings

   your *(m pl)* heads/beginnings

b. your *(m sg)* hand

   their hand

   their hands

   his hand

her hand

her hands

c. your *(m sg)* face

her face/its face/its surface

your *(m pl)* face/faces

his face/its face/its surface

their faces/surfaces

our faces

d. his spirit

her spirit

our spirit

our spirits

their spirit

their spirits

e. your *(m sg)* friend/neighbor/companion/fellow human being

his friend/neighbor/companion/fellow human being

his friends/neighbors/companions/fellow human beings

your *(m pl)* friends/neighbors/companions/fellow human beings

their friends/neighbors/companions/fellow human beings

their friend/neighbor/companion/fellow human being

f. *(Remember that there are two words in Hebrew for heart:* לֵב *and* לֵבָב*.)*

your *(m sg)* heart

your *(m sg)* heart

their heart

their heart

their hearts

their hearts

Exercise 2 [page 72]

Form	Root	Plural	Singular
perfect	י־שׁ־ב	יָשְׁבוּ	הָיָה
perfect	א־מ־ר	אָמְרוּ	הָיְתָה
participle	ב־נ־ה	בּוֹנִים	יִהְיֶה
participle	א־מ־ר	אוֹמְרִים	בָּנָה
participle	י־שׁ־ב	יוֹשְׁבוֹת	בּוֹנֶה
imperfect	א־מ־ר	יֹאמְרוּ	יִבְנֶה
perfect	י־ד־ע	יָדְעוּ	יָשְׁבָה
perfect	ב־נ־ה	בָּנוּ	יוֹשֵׁב
participle	י־ד־ע	יוֹדְעִים	יוֹשֶׁבֶת
perfect	ה־י־ה	הָיוּ	אָמַר
imperfect	ב־נ־ה	יִבְנוּ	יֹאמַר
participle	י־שׁ־ב	יוֹשְׁבִים	אוֹמֵר
imperfect	ה־י־ה	יִהְיוּ	יָדְעָה
perfect	ה־י־ה	הָיוּ	יוֹדֵעַ

Notes on

CHAPTER 7 UNIT FOUR

Torah Study Text: Genesis 12:1–7 [page 76]

Following are all the words, roots, endings, and prefixes appearing in Genesis 12:1–7 that have already been introduced. The book and chapter in which they were introduced is indicated in parentheses.

¹וַיֹּאמֶר יְהֹוָה אֶל־אַבְרָם לֶךְ־לְךָ מֵאַרְצְךָ וּמִמּוֹלַדְתְּךָ וּמִבֵּית אָבִיךָ
אֶל־הָאָרֶץ אֲשֶׁר אַרְאֶךָּ: ²וְאֶעֶשְׂךָ לְגוֹי גָּדוֹל וַאֲבָרֶכְךָ וַאֲגַדְּלָה
שְׁמֶךָ וֶהְיֵה בְּרָכָה: ³וַאֲבָרְכָה מְבָרְכֶיךָ וּמְקַלֶּלְךָ אָאֹר וְנִבְרְכוּ בְךָ
כֹּל מִשְׁפְּחֹת הָאֲדָמָה: ⁴וַיֵּלֶךְ אַבְרָם כַּאֲשֶׁר דִּבֶּר אֵלָיו יְהֹוָה וַיֵּלֶךְ
אִתּוֹ לוֹט וְאַבְרָם בֶּן־חָמֵשׁ שָׁנִים וְשִׁבְעִים שָׁנָה בְּצֵאתוֹ מֵחָרָן:
⁵וַיִּקַּח אַבְרָם אֶת־שָׂרַי אִשְׁתּוֹ וְאֶת־לוֹט בֶּן־אָחִיו וְאֶת־כָּל־רְכוּשָׁם
אֲשֶׁר רָכָשׁוּ וְאֶת־הַנֶּפֶשׁ אֲשֶׁר־עָשׂוּ בְחָרָן וַיֵּצְאוּ לָלֶכֶת אַרְצָה
כְּנַעַן וַיָּבֹאוּ אַרְצָה כְּנָעַן: ⁶וַיַּעֲבֹר אַבְרָם בָּאָרֶץ עַד מְקוֹם שְׁכֶם
עַד אֵלוֹן מוֹרֶה וְהַכְּנַעֲנִי אָז בָּאָרֶץ: ⁷וַיֵּרָא יְהֹוָה אֶל־אַבְרָם וַיֹּאמֶר
לְזַרְעֲךָ אֶתֵּן אֶת־הָאָרֶץ הַזֹּאת וַיִּבֶן שָׁם מִזְבֵּחַ לַיהֹוָה הַנִּרְאֶה
אֵלָיו:

say, utter, tell *(B.I.F.B. Ch 1)* appears in the word וַיֹּאמֶר	—	א־מ־ר
reversing vav, *may also be translated as* and:	—	וַ־, וְ־

וַיֹּאמֶר, וְנִבְרְכוּ, וַיֵּלֶךְ, וַיִּקַּח, וַיֵּצְאוּ, וַיָּבֹאוּ, וַיַּעֲבֹר, וַיֵּרָא, וַיִּבֶן

and *(attached prefix) (A.I.E. Ch 2), appears on the following words:*	—	וְ־, וּ־

וּמִמּוֹלַדְתְּךָ, וּמִבֵּית, וְאֶעֶשְׂךָ, וַאֲבָרֶכְךָ, וַאֲגַדְּלָה, וֶהְיֵה,
וַאֲבָרְכָה, וּמְקַלֶּלְךָ, וְאַבְרָם, וְשִׁבְעִים, וְאֶת, וְהַכְּנַעֲנִי

to, toward *(B.I.F.B. Ch 3)*	—	אֶל

-לְ   to, for *(attached preposition) (A.I.E. Ch 8)*, appears on the
following words: —

לְךָ, לְגוֹי, לָלֶכֶת, לְזַרְעֶךָ, לַיהוָה

ךָ-   your, you *(attached ending) m sg (A.I.E. Ch 6)*, appears on
the following words: —

לְךָ, מֵאַרְצְךָ, וּמִמּוֹלַדְתְּךָ, אָבִיךָ, אַרְאֶךָ, וְאֶעֶשְׂךָ, וַאֲבָרֶכְךָ,
שְׁמֶךָ, מְבָרֲכֶיךָ, וּמְקַלֶּלְךָ, בְּךָ, לְזַרְעֶךָ

אֶרֶץ   earth, land *f (A.I.E. Ch 3)* —

(אֶרֶץ *becomes* אָרֶץ *when the prefix* הָ *the is attached*)

מִ-, מֵי-   from, than *(attached preposition) (A.I.E. Ch 10)*, appears on
the following words: —

מֵאַרְצְךָ, וּמִמּוֹלַדְתְּךָ, וּמִבֵּית, מֵחָרָן

בֵּית   *word-pair form of* בַּיִת, house *m*
(A.I.E. Ch 6) —

אָבִיךָ   אָב, father, ancestor *m (A.I.E. Ch 5), with*
pronoun ending —

הַ-, הָ-   the *(attached prefix) (A.I.E. Ch 1)*, appears on the
following words: —

הָאָרֶץ, הָאֲדָמָה, הַנֶּפֶשׁ, וְהַכְּנַעֲנִי, הַזֹּאת, הַנִּרְאֶה

אֲשֶׁר   who, that, which *(A.I.E. Ch 8)* —

ע-שׂ-ה   make, do, act *(A.I.E. Ch 7), appears in the following*
words: וְאֶעֶשְׂךָ, עָשׂוּ —

גּוֹי   nation, people *m (A.I.E. Ch 8)* —

גָּדוֹל   big, great *adj (A.I.E. Ch 5)* —

ב-ר-ך   bless *(A.I.E. Ch 1), appears in the*
folowing words: —

וַאֲבָרֶכְךָ, בְּרָכָה, וַאֲבָרְכָה, מְבָרֲכֶיךָ, וְנִבְרְכוּ

שְׁמֶךָ   שֵׁם, name *m (A.I.E. Ch 1), with*
pronoun ending —

ה-י-ה   be, exist *(B.I.F.B. Ch 1), appears in the*
word וְהְיֵה —

בְּ-, בְ-   with, in *(attached preposition) (A.I.E. Ch 6)*, appears on the
following words: —

בְּךָ, בְּצֵאתוֹ, בְחָרָן, בָּאָרֶץ

all, every *(A.I.E. Ch 8)*	—	כֹּל, כָּל
plural of מִשְׁפָּחָה, family *f* *(A.I.E. Ch 8)*	—	מִשְׁפָּחֹת
earth, ground, land *f (A.I.E. Ch 8)*	—	אֲדָמָה
speak, talk *(A.I.E. Ch 6)*, appears in *the word* דִּבֶּר	—	ד-ב-ר
his, him *(attached ending) m sg (A.I.E. Ch 9)*, *appears on the following words:*	—	־וֹ, ־יו

אֵלָיו, אִתּוֹ, בְּצֵאתוֹ, אִשְׁתּוֹ, אָחִיו

אֵת, with *(preposition) (B.I.F.B. Ch 3)*, *with pronoun ending attached*	—	אִתּוֹ
son, child *m (A.I.E. Ch 3)*	—	בֵּן
go out, come out *(A.I.E. Ch 10)*, appears in the following *words:* בְּצֵאתוֹ, וַיֵּצְאוּ	—	י-צ-א
definite direct object marker (untranslatable) (A.I.E. Ch 4), appears five times in our Torah Study Text	—	אֵת
אִשָּׁה, woman, wife *f (B.I.F.B. Ch 3), with pronoun ending attached*	—	אִשְׁתּוֹ
אָח, brother *m (B.I.F.B. Ch 3), with pronoun ending attached*	—	אָחִיו
their, them *(attached ending) (B.I.F.B. Ch 6), appears on the word* רְכוּשָׁם	—	־ָם
soul, mind, breath *f (A.I.E. Ch 6)*	—	נֶפֶשׁ
give, grant, permit *(A.I.E. Ch 4), appears in the word* אֶתֵּן	—	נ-ת-ן
build *(B.I.F.B. Ch 5), appears in the word* וַיִּבֶן	—	ב-נ-ה
there *(B.I.F.B. Ch 5)*	—	שָׁם

Translating the Torah Study Text [pages 76–79]

As your students work on their translations, the following comments may assist them:

1. Prepositions do not always translate smoothly from one language to another, as with the ל in verse 2: וְאֶעֶשְׂךָ לְגוֹי גָּדוֹל, "and I will make you **to/for** a great nation."

2. The translations provided underneath each verb do not give all the possible ways of

translating the verb. For example, in verse 4, the translation under the perfect verb דִּבֶּר is simply "spoke," though, as a perfect verb, it could be translated as "did speak," "had spoken," and so forth. It is, in fact, the last meaning that is understood by all four of our translations cited.

3. The subject of a verb may not appear immediately after the verb. They may be separated by a preposition, as in verse 4: כַּאֲשֶׁר דִּבֶּר אֵלָיו יְהֹוָה, "as the Eternal had spoken to him," or אִתּוֹ לוֹט וַיֵּלֶךְ, "and Lot went with him."

4. As indicated in the notes to the new Vocabulary on page 81, בֶּן...שָׁנִים is a Hebrew idiom meaning "...*years old.*" This idiom appears in verse 4.

[pages 79–81]

Following are some variations among our four translations that you may wish to point out to your students.

The JPS translation provides the essential meaning of God's words to Abram in the first verse, but it condenses the Hebrew, rendering מֵאַרְצְךָ וּמִמּוֹלַדְתְּךָ, "from your land and from your birthplace/kin," as a single concept: "from your native land." The other three translations all preserve the repetitive nature of the Hebrew, providing three separate terms in the English for each of the three items appearing in the Hebrew: מֵאַרְצְךָ וּמִמּוֹלַדְתְּךָ וּמִבֵּית אָבִיךָ.

Everett Fox's translation attempts to give the English reader a feel for the rhythms, repetitions, and wordplays in the Hebrew. Notice, for example, how he sets up all of God's speech to Abram in verses 1 through 3 in poetic form and how he hypenates in verse 2 "give-you-blessing," showing that these words are all representing a single Hebrew word וַאֲבָרֶכְךָ. Also notice how his is the only one of our four translations that renders מִזְבֵּח, "altar," in verse 7 as "slaughter-site," which preserves in English the meaning of the root ז־ב־ח, "slaughter for sacrifice."

A detail in the Hebrew that has given rise to midrashic interpretation is the phrase in verse 5 וְאֶת־הַנֶּפֶשׁ אֲשֶׁר־עָשׂוּ בְחָרָן, "the soul that they made in Haran." According to the classical midrash *B'reishit Rabbah* 39:14, Abram and Sarai "made souls" in Haran by proselytizing. The ArtScroll *Chumash* provides the most literal translation of this verse: "the souls they had made in Haran," which is in keeping with the midrashic interpretation. The *Jerusalem Bible* and the JPS translation both render the perfect verb עָשׂוּ as "they had acquired," though the root ע־שׂ־ה doesn't actually mean "acquire," but "make," "do," or "act." Everett Fox provides a translation that attempts to preserve the meaning of the Hebrew root: "the persons whom they had made-their-own in Harran."

Vocabulary [page 81]

All the new vocabulary words are identified and highlighted within the Torah Study Text at the beginning of Chapter 8, on page 89.

1. The plural of the word שָׁנָה, "year," is שָׁנִים. Each form appears once in the Torah Study Text.

2. The word כְּנַעַן, "Canaan," appears twice. It also appears in verse 6 with prefixes and suffixes in the form וְהַכְּנַעֲנִי, "and the Canaanite."

3. The word זֶרַע, "seed/offspring," appears only once, in verse 7, with a prefix and a suffix: לְזַרְעֲךָ, "to your seed/offspring."

Hebrew Root Review [pages 82–83]

As it is helpful for students to notice variations caused by certain root letters, you may wish to point out that there are variations caused by the final root letter ה in the participle forms of the last two roots: ח־י־ה and צ־ו־ה. Remind your students that this type of variation has already appeared in the participle forms of the פָּעַל roots ב־נ־ה and ע־שׂ־ה. The feminine singular participle has an ◌ָה ending instead of ◌ֶ◌ֶת (מְצַוָּה, בּוֹנָה), and the final ה drops out in the plural forms.

The Hebrew root ב־ר־ך appears four times in our Torah Study Text:

1. וַאֲבָרֶכְךָ—a פָּעֵל imperfect אֲנִי, "I," form with reversing *vav* and pronoun ending attached

2. בְּרָכָה—a noun meaning "blessing"

3. וַאֲבָרְכָה—a פָּעֵל imperfect אֲנִי, "I," form with reversing *vav* attached

4. מְבָרְכֶיךָ—a פָּעֵל *masculine plural* participle with pronoun ending attached

5. וְנִבְרְכוּ—a נִפְעַל (verb pattern not yet introduced) perfect plural form with reversing *vav*

Exercises

Exercise 2 [page 85]

2. Draw a line connecting each Hebrew word to its English translation. For some words, there can be more than one correct translation.

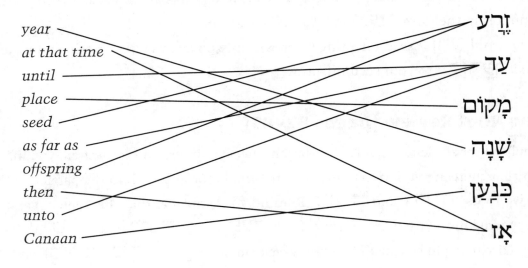

year	זֶרַע
at that time	עַד
until	מָקוֹם
place	שָׁנָה
seed	כְּנַעַן
as far as	אָז
offspring	
then	
unto	
Canaan	

Exercise 3 [page 85]

3. The following are plural forms of words introduced as vocabulary in this chapter. Draw a line connecting each plural word to its singular form. Translate both into English.

places _____	מְקוֹמוֹת	שָׁנָה	year _____
seeds, offspring _____	זְרָעִים	מָקוֹם	place _____
years _____	שָׁנִים	זֶרַע	seed, offspring _____

Exercise 4 [page 86]

a. your *(m sg)* seed/offspring

his seed/offspring

her seed/offspring

your *(m pl)* seed/offspring

their seed/offspring

b. the land of Canaan

the king of Canaan

the people/nation of Canaan

the inhabitants of Canaan

the sons/children of Canaan (*i.e.,* the Canaanites)

c. his place

his places

our place

our places

their place

d. in one year

in every year

the days of the year

the head/beginning of the year (Rosh HaShanah)

many years

e. until evening

until morning

until/unto eternity

until/as far as there

from the city until/as far as the water

f. then/at that time

from then (*i.e.,* since then)

then/at that time in Canaan

then/at that time in the land

then/at that time in Jerusalem

Exercise 5 [page 87]

Translation	Root	Participle
sanctify *m sg*	ק־ד־שׁ	מְקַדֵּשׁ
praise *f sg*	ה־ל־ל	מְהַלֶּלֶת
bless *m sg*	ב־ר־ך	מְבָרֵךְ
give life *m sg*	ח־י־ה	מְחַיֶּה
give life *f sg*	ח־י־ה	מְחַיָּה
command *m sg*	צ־ו־ה	מְצַוֶּה
command *f sg*	צ־ו־ה	מְצַוָּה
speak *f pl*	ד־ב־ר	מְדַבְּרוֹת
speak *m sg*	ד־ב־ר	מְדַבֵּר
command *m pl*	צ־ו־ה	מְצַוִּים
bless *m pl*	ב־ר־ך	מְבָרְכִים
sanctify *m pl*	ק־ד־שׁ	מְקַדְּשִׁים
praise *f pl*	ה־ל־ל	מְהַלְלוֹת
sanctify *f sg*	ק־ד־שׁ	מְקַדֶּשֶׁת
praise *m sg*	ה־ל־ל	מְהַלֵּל
bless *f sg*	ב־ר־ך	מְבָרֶכֶת

Notes on

Torah Study Text: Vocabulary and Root Review [page 89]

Vocabulary words that appear in our Torah Study Text in variant forms or with prefixes or suffixes attached were noted in the Vocabulary section of the previous chapter of this Teacher's Guide. The word הַכְּנַעֲנִי, "the Canaanite," in verse 6 is derived from the new vocabulary word כְּנַעַן, "Canaan." The various forms of the root ב־ר־ך were explained on page 56 in this Teacher's Guide.

Building Blocks:
The פִּעֵל (Pi-el) Pattern [pages 90–91]

If you have students who are interested in grammatical details, you may want to turn back to the participle chart in the Hebrew Root Review section of Chapter 7, on page 82 in the text, and to the Grammar Enrichment charts of this chapter, on page 92 of the text, to point out certain characteristics of the פִּעֵל pattern:

1. Though not mentioned in our text, verbs in the פִּעֵל pattern have a *dageish*, a dot, in the middle root letter of all forms (perfect, participle, and imperfect). The only exception is when the middle root letter is one of the "throaty" five (laryngeal) letters— א, ה, ח, ע, ר —in which a *dageish* cannot be placed. The variations in the vowels of the root ב־ר־ך (as opposed to the roots ק־ד־שׁ, ה־ל־ל, and ד־ב־ר) are caused by the fact that the middle root letter is ר, one of these "throaty" five letters.

2. The פִּעֵל pattern has a characteristic vowel pattern, ▓ ▪ ▪ ▓, which appears in both the *masculine singular* participle form and in the הוּא and הִיא imperfect forms. The plural participles and imperfect plural forms follow the same characteristic vowel pattern, with plural endings instead of the ▓ vowel.

We have introduced roots thus far appearing in either the פָּעַל pattern or the פִּעֵל pattern. It is possible, however, for a Hebrew root to appear in more than one verb pattern. If the same root appears in both the פָּעַל and the פִּעֵל patterns, it will have a related, but different, meaning in each pattern. The meaning in the פִּעֵל pattern may be an intensification of the פָּעַל meaning. Following are examples from some familiar and unfamiliar roots:

Meaning in פִּעֵל	Meaning in פָּעַל	Root
send away, release	send	שׁ־ל־ח
shatter, smash	break	שׁ־ב־ר
teach	study, learn	ל־מ־ד
desire, covet	love	א־ה־ב
preserve, conserve	guard, keep	שׁ־מ־ר

[pages 92–93]

See notes on the characteristics of the פִּעֵל pattern in the Building Blocks section above. The plural perfect form צִוּוּ looks very strange to most students. Explain that the first *vav* is a consonant *v* with the *dageish*, dot, characteristic of the פִּעֵל pattern, inserted. The second *vav* is the vowel *oo*. The word is pronounced *tsi-vu*. The same is true for the plural imperfect form יְצַוּוּ, pronounced *y'tsa-vu*.

Additional Reading and Translation Practice [pages 93–98]

1. Shabbat candle lighting blessing can be found in the gender-sensitive *Gates of Prayer* on page 38.

2. מִי שֶׁבֵּרַךְ can be found in the 1998 CCAR *Rabbi's Manual* on pages 195–196.

3. בְּרֹאשׁ הַשָּׁנָה can be found in *Gates of Repentance* on page 108.

4. These words to mourners can be found in the 1998 CCAR *Rabbi's Manual* on page 162.

5. Psalm 148:13–14 can be found in the gender-sensitive *Gates of Prayer* on page 146.

6. Numbers 6:24–26 (the Priestly Benediction) can be found in *On the Doorposts of Your House* on page 40.

7. אַשְׁרֵי can be found in the gender-sensitive *Gates of Prayer* on pages 125–127.

Exercises

Exercise 1 [page 99]

Translation	Root	Form	Verb	Pronoun
sanctify	שׁ־ד־ק	participle	מְקַדֵּשׁ	
speak	ד־ב־ר	participle	מְדַבְּרִים	
bless	ב־ר־ך	participle	מְבָרֶכֶת	הוּא—he
give life	ח־י־ה	participle	מְחַיֶּה	
commanded	צ־ו־ה	perfect	צִוָּה	
praised	ה־ל־ל	perfect	הִלֵּל	
spoke	ד־ב־ר	perfect	דִּבְּרָה	הִיא—she
blessed	ב־ר־ך	perfect	בֵּרְכָה	
sanctified	ק־ד־שׁ	perfect	קִדְּשׁוּ	
will/may bless	ב־ר־ך	imperfect	תְּבָרֵךְ	
will/may praise	ה־ל־ל	imperfect	יְהַלְלוּ	הֵם—they
will/may command	צ־ו־ה	imperfect	יְצַוּוּ	
will/may give life	ח־י־ה	imperfect	יְחַיֶּה	

Torah Study Text: Genesis 22:1–5, 9–12 [pages 102–103]

Following are all the words, roots, endings, and prefixes appearing in Genesis 22:1–5, 22:9–12 that have already been introduced. The book and chapter in which they were introduced is indicated in parentheses.

Genesis 22:1–5

וַיְהִי אַחַר הַדְּבָרִים הָאֵלֶּה וְהָאֱלֹהִים נִסָּה אֶת־אַבְרָהָם וַיֹּאמֶר ¹
אֵלָיו אַבְרָהָם וַיֹּאמֶר הִנֵּנִי: ²וַיֹּאמֶר קַח־נָא אֶת־בִּנְךָ אֶת־יְחִידְךָ
אֲשֶׁר־אָהַבְתָּ אֶת־יִצְחָק וְלֶךְ־לְךָ אֶל־אֶרֶץ הַמֹּרִיָּה וְהַעֲלֵהוּ שָׁם
לְעֹלָה עַל אַחַד הֶהָרִים אֲשֶׁר אֹמַר אֵלֶיךָ: ³וַיַּשְׁכֵּם אַבְרָהָם בַּבֹּקֶר
וַיַּחֲבֹשׁ אֶת־חֲמֹרוֹ וַיִּקַּח אֶת־שְׁנֵי נְעָרָיו אִתּוֹ וְאֵת יִצְחָק בְּנוֹ וַיְבַקַּע
עֲצֵי עֹלָה וַיָּקָם וַיֵּלֶךְ אֶל־הַמָּקוֹם אֲשֶׁר־אָמַר־לוֹ הָאֱלֹהִים: ⁴בַּיּוֹם
הַשְּׁלִישִׁי וַיִּשָּׂא אַבְרָהָם אֶת־עֵינָיו וַיַּרְא אֶת־הַמָּקוֹם מֵרָחֹק:
⁵וַיֹּאמֶר אַבְרָהָם אֶל־נְעָרָיו שְׁבוּ־לָכֶם פֹּה עִם־הַחֲמוֹר....

Genesis 22:9–12

⁹וַיָּבֹאוּ אֶל־הַמָּקוֹם אֲשֶׁר אָמַר־לוֹ הָאֱלֹהִים וַיִּבֶן שָׁם אַבְרָהָם
אֶת־הַמִּזְבֵּחַ וַיַּעֲרֹךְ אֶת־הָעֵצִים וַיַּעֲקֹד אֶת־יִצְחָק בְּנוֹ וַיָּשֶׂם אֹתוֹ
עַל־הַמִּזְבֵּחַ מִמַּעַל לָעֵצִים: ¹⁰וַיִּשְׁלַח אַבְרָהָם אֶת־יָדוֹ וַיִּקַּח
אֶת־הַמַּאֲכֶלֶת לִשְׁחֹט אֶת־בְּנוֹ: ¹¹וַיִּקְרָא אֵלָיו מַלְאַךְ יְהֹוָה
מִן־הַשָּׁמַיִם וַיֹּאמֶר אַבְרָהָם אַבְרָהָם וַיֹּאמֶר הִנֵּנִי: ¹²וַיֹּאמֶר
אַל־תִּשְׁלַח יָדְךָ אֶל־הַנַּעַר....

be, exist *(B.I.F.B. Ch 1)*, appears in the
word וַיְהִי — הָיָה

reversing vav, *may also be translated as*
and: — וַ

וַיְהִי, וַיֹּאמֶר, וַיַּשְׁכֵּם, וַיַּחֲבֹשׁ, וַיִּקַּח, וַיְבַקַּע, וַיָּקָם, וַיֵּלֶךְ, וַיִּשָּׂא,
וַיַּרְא, וַיָּבֹאוּ, וַיִּבֶן, וַיַּעֲרֹךְ, וַיַּעֲקֹד, וַיָּשֶׂם, וַיִּשְׁלַח, וַיִּקְרָא

word, speech *(A.I.E. Ch 10) m;* thing
(B.I.F.B. Ch 9) — דָּבָר

the *(attached prefix) (A.I.E. Ch 1)*, appears on the
following words: — הַ, הָ

הַדְּבָרִים, הָאֵלֶּה, וְהָאֱלֹהִים, הַמֹּרִיָּה, הֶהָרִים, הַמָּקוֹם, הָאֱלֹהִים,
הַשְּׁלִישִׁי, הַחֲמוֹר, הַמִּזְבֵּחַ, הָעֵצִים, הַמַּאֲכֶלֶת, הַשָּׁמַיִם, הַנַּעַר

plural ending *(A.I.E. Ch 2)*, appears on the
following words: — ־ים

הַדְּבָרִים, הֶהָרִים, הָעֵצִים, לָעֵצִים

God *m (A.I.E. Ch 4)* — אֱלֹהִים

and *(attached prefix) (A.I.E. Ch 2)*, appears on the
following words: — וְ, וּ

וְהָאֱלֹהִים, וְלֶךְ, וְהַעֲלֵהוּ

Abraham *(A.I.E. Ch 5)* — אַבְרָהָם

say, utter, tell *(B.I.F.B. Ch 1)* appears in the following
words: וַיֹּאמֶר, אֹמַר, אָמַר — אָמַר

to, toward *(B.I.F.B. Ch 3)* — אֶל

his, him *(attached ending) m sg (A.I.E. Ch 9)*, appears on the
following words: — ־וֹ, ־יו

אֵלָיו, חֲמֹרוֹ, נְעָרָיו, אִתּוֹ, בְּנוֹ, לוֹ, עֵינָיו, אֹתוֹ, יָדוֹ

*definite direct object marker (untranslatable) (A.I.E. Ch 4), appears
sixteen times in our Torah Study Text, including once with a
pronoun ending attached:* אֹתוֹ — אֶת

son, child *m (A.I.E. Ch 3)*, appears with pronoun
ending attached — בֵּן

your, you *(attached ending) m sg (A.I.E. Ch 6)*, appears on
the following words: — ־ךָ

בִּנְךָ, יְחִידְךָ, לְךָ, אֵלֶיךָ, יָדְךָ

who, that, which *(A.I.E. Ch 8)* — אֲשֶׁר

love *(A.I.E. Ch 6)* appears in the word אָהַבְתָּ	—	א־ה־ב
Isaac *(A.I.E. Ch 5)*	—	יִצְחָק
earth, land *f (A.I.E. Ch 3)*	—	אֶרֶץ
him, it *(attached ending) m sg (A.I.E. Ch 9)*, appears on the word וְהַעֲלֵהוּ	—	־הוּ
there *(B.I.F.B. Ch 5)*	—	שָׁם
to, for *(attached preposition) (A.I.E. Ch 8)*, appears on the following words:	—	לְ־

לְךָ, לְעֹלָה, לָכֶם, לוֹ, לָעֵצִים, לִשְׁחֹט

on, about *(A.I.E. Ch 8)*	—	עַל
one *m (B.I.F.B. Ch 5)*	—	אַחַד
morning *m (B.I.F.B. Ch 1)*	—	בֹּקֶר
with, in *(attached preposition) (A.I.E. Ch 6)*, appears on the following words: בַּבֹּקֶר, בַּיּוֹם	—	בְּ־
day *m (A.I.E. Ch 3)*	—	יוֹם
from, than *(attached preposition) (A.I.E. Ch 10)*, appears on the following words:	—	מִ־, מִי־

מֵרָחֹק, מִמַּעַל

sit, settle, dwell *(B.I.F.B. Ch 5)*, appears in the word שְׁבוּ	—	י־ש־ב
your, you *(attached ending) m pl (A.I.E. Ch 6)*, appears on the word לָכֶם	—	־כֶם
build *(B.I.F.B. Ch 5)*, appears in the word וַיִּבֶן	—	ב־נ־ה
hand *f (A.I.E. Ch 6)*, appears with pronoun ending attached	—	יָד
angel, messenger *m (A.I.E. Ch 6)*	—	מַלְאַךְ
heavens, sky *m (A.I.E. Ch 3)*	—	שָׁמַיִם

Translating the Torah Study Text [pages 103–105]

As your students work on their translations, the following comments may assist them:

1. The word דָּבָר, appearing in the plural in verse 1, was introduced in Chapter 10 of *Aleph Isn't Enough* with the meaning "word/speech." It can also mean "thing." The first Torah commentary, from *Tanchuma*, presented in this chapter on page 112 takes as its point of departure the double meaning of this word.

2. Demonstrative pronouns (i.e., this, that, these) can act as adjectives in Hebrew, coming after the noun. An example of this appears in verse 1: הַדְּבָרִים הָאֵלֶּה, "these things/words."

   Demonstrative pronouns are introduced and further explained in *Tav Is for Torah*, Chapter 2.

3. The words לֶךְ־לְךָ (literally: "go to/for you") are a biblical idiom. This idiom appeared in our last Torah Study Text, in Genesis 12:1, and it appears in this text in verse 2. In the last Torah Study Text, in Chapter 7, it was translated by our various translators as "go forth," "go for yourself," "go-you-forth," and "get thee out." In this passage, two of our translations (JPS and the ArtScroll *Chumash*) render it simply as "go," while Fox uses the same translation he used in Genesis 12:1, "go-you-forth," and the *Jerusalem Bible* says "get thee."

4. In Hebrew, numbers can be used in word pairs, as in verse 2, אַחַד הֶהָרִים, "one of the mountains," or in verse 3, שְׁנֵי נְעָרָיו, which can be translated either "two of his lads/young men" or "his two lads/young men."

[pages 105–109]

The JPS translation aims to provide an idiomatic English translation. In so doing, however, some of the small details of the Hebrew text, which can sound awkward when translated literally, are obscured or omitted. These details are generally not significant in terms of relating the basic Torah narrative. They can, however, be significant in terms of Torah commentary, which is so often built upon the small details of the Hebrew text. You may wish to point out to your students some examples in our Torah Study Text:

1. As noted above, the double meaning of the word דְּבָרִים, "words/things," in verse 1 gives rise to the first Torah commentary cited in this chapter. The other three translations preserve this word, rendering it as either "things" or "events": "And it happened after these things" (ArtScroll *Chumash*), "Now after these it events it was" (Fox), and

"And it came to pass after these things" (*Jerusalem Bible*). The JPS translation omits this word altogether, rendering the opening phrase as "Some time afterward."

2. Verse 3 begins with the words וַיַּשְׁכֵּם אַבְרָהָם בַּבֹּקֶר, in which Abraham is the subject: "Abraham rose early in the morning." The other three translations keep Abraham as the subject, though they translate the verb slightly differently. Only the JPS translation omits Abraham altogether in its translation of this phrase: "So early next morning." Abraham's decision to get up early in the morning is a key detail in the midrash from *Tanchuma* included as the last Torah commentary in this chapter.

3. There are a pair of verbs in verse 3: וַיָּקָם וַיֵּלֶךְ, "and [he] arose and went." The JPS translation combines the two verbs into a single statement: "and he set out." The other three translations render the two verbs separately, with the ArtScroll *Chumash* providing the most awkwardly literal translation: "[he] stood up and went."

   Another pair of verbs appear in verse 10: וַיִּשְׁלַח אַבְרָהָם אֶת־יָדוֹ וַיִּקַּח אֶת־הַמַּאֲכֶלֶת, "Abraham **stretched out** his hand and **took** the knife." The other three translations include two verbs here, while the JPS translation combines them into a single statement: "And Abraham picked up the knife."

4. In verse 4, Abraham's eyes are mentioned: וַיִּשָּׂא אַבְרָהָם אֶת עֵינָיו, "Abraham lifted his eyes."

   The mention of Abraham's eyes is retained in the other three translations, while the JPS translation treats this expression as an idiom and translates it with a comparable English idiom: "Abraham looked up."

Vocabulary [page 109]

All the new vocabulary words are identified and highlighted within the Torah Study Text at the beginning of Chapter 10, on page 118.

1. The word הִנֵּה, "behold/here [is]," appears in verses 1 and 11 with the יִ, "me," pronoun ending attached. This pronoun ending was included in the Grammar Enrichment chart of Chapter 9 of *Aleph Isn't Enough*, but it will be formally introduced as a Building Block in *Tav Is for Torah*, Chapter 4.

2. The word הַר, "mountain/mount," appears only in the plural form: הֶהָרִים, "the mountains."

3. The word עֵץ, "tree/wood," appears only as a plural: הָעֵצִים, לָעֵצִים, or in the plural word-pair form: עֲצֵי.

4. The word עַיִן, "eye," appears only as a plural, with pronoun ending attached: עֵינָיו, "his eyes."

5. The word נַעַר appears once with the definite article, הַנַּעַר, "the lad," and twice as a plural with pronoun ending attached, נְעָרָיו, "his lads/young men."

The Hebrew Root [pages 109–111]

The Hebrew root ע־ל־ה is a final ה root, hence its forms contain the same irregularities as other final ה roots, such as ב־נ־ה. It contains additional variations in the imperfect, caused by its first root letter ע. All of these variations are identical to those found in the forms of the root ע־שׂ־ה, another first-letter ע and final-letter ה root.

The verb from the root ע־ל־ה that appears in verse 2, וְהַעֲלֵהוּ, is a הִפְעִיל command form with a pronoun ending attached. The הִפְעִיל verb pattern will be introduced as a Building Block in the next chapter.

The perfect forms of the root ה־ל־ך are regular, but the imperfect forms have the same irregularity as first letter י roots, such as י־שׁ־ב and י־צ־א, with the first root letter dropping out. The form וַיֵּלֶךְ in verse 3 is an imperfect הוּא form with a reversing vav. The form לֵךְ in verse 2 is a command form.

Exercises

Exercise 2 [page 114]

2. Draw a line connecting each Hebrew word to its English translation. For some words, there can be more than one correct translation.

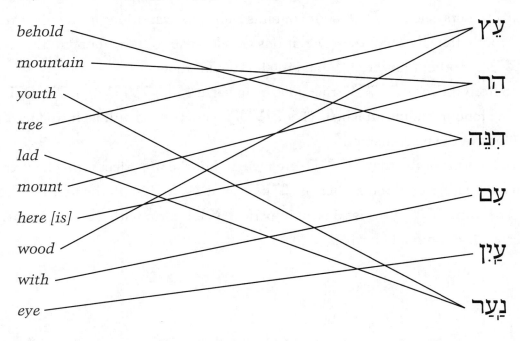

behold	עֵץ
mountain	הַר
youth	הִנֵּה
tree	עִם
lad	עַיִן
mount	נַעַר
here [is]	
wood	
with	
eye	

Exercise 3 [page 114]

3. The following are plural forms of words introduced as vocabulary in this chapter. Draw a line connecting each plural word to its singular form. Translate both into English.

trees/wood	עֵצִים	הַר	mount/mountain
mountains	הָרִים	נַעַר	lad/youth/young man
eyes	עֵינַיִם	עַיִן	eye
lads/youths/young men	נְעָרִים	עֵץ	tree/wood

Exercise 4 [page 115]

a. his eye

his eyes

our eyes

your eyes

their eyes

b. your *(m sg)* lad

your *(m pl)* lad

your *(m pl)* lads

their lad

their lads

c. with us

with him/it

with her/it

with you *(m pl)*

with them

d. behold you *(m sg)* *or* here you *(m sg)* are

behold him/it *or* here he/it is

behold us *or* here we are

behold you *(m pl)* *or* here you *(m pl)* are

behold them *or* here they are

e. the mount/mountain of God

[the] mount/mountain of [the] house of God

Mount Zion

the mount of holiness *(i.e., the Holy Mountain, the Temple Mount in Jerusalem)*

the top of the mountain

f. a good tree *or* good wood

one tree

wood and stone

the tree of life

a tree of fruit, a fruit tree

Exercise 5 [pages 115–116]

Translation	Root	Participle
make, do *m sg*	ע־שׂ־ה	עוֹשֶׂה
go up, ascend *m sg*	ע־ל־ה	עוֹלֶה
go up, ascend *f sg*	ע־ל־ה	עוֹלָה
build *m pl*	ב־נ־ה	בּוֹנִים
know *m pl*	י־ד־ע	יוֹדְעִים
sit, dwell *m pl*	י־שׁ־ב	יוֹשְׁבִים
bless *m pl*	ב־ר־ך	מְבָרְכִים
praise *f pl*	ה־ל־ל	מְהַלְלוֹת
walk, go *m sg*	ה־ל־ך	הוֹלֵךְ
walk, go *f sg*	ה־ל־ך	הוֹלֶכֶת
sit, dwell *f pl*	י־שׁ־ב	יוֹשְׁבוֹת
choose *m pl*	ב־ח־ר	בּוֹחֲרִים
work, serve *f pl*	ע־ב־ד	עוֹבְדוֹת
sanctify *m sg*	ק־ד־שׁ	מְקַדֵּשׁ
command *m sg*	צ־ו־ה	מְצַוֶּה
say, tell *f sg*	א־מ־ר	אוֹמֶרֶת

Notes on

Torah Study Text: Vocabulary and Root Review
[page 118]

Vocabulary words that appear in our Torah Study Text in variant forms or with prefixes or suffixes attached were noted in the Vocabulary section of the previous chapter of this Teacher's Guide. The various forms of the new roots הָלַךְ and עָלָה were explained in the Hebrew Root section of the previous chapter of this Teacher's Guide.

Building Blocks

Different Verb Patterns [pages 119–121]

As mentioned on page 63 of this Teacher's Guide, [in the Building Blocks—*Pi-el* Pattern section of Chapter 8], the same root can appear in both the פָּעַל and פִּעֵל patterns. When it does, the meaning in the פִּעֵל pattern may be an intensification of the פָּעַל meaning.

Torah Study Text with Building Blocks [page 121]

וַיַּשְׁכֵּם, "[he] rose early," is an example of a verb that does *not* have a causative meaning in the הִפְעִיל pattern.

[page 122]

The final root letter ה causes the same variations in the הִפְעִיל pattern as it causes in the פָּעַל and פִּעֵל verb patterns. You may want to look at the various forms (participle, perfect, and imperfect) of the roots חָיָה and עָלָה in the הִפְעִיל verb charts at the back of the textbook.

These final ה verbs do not contain the יִ vowel between the second and third root letters, generally characteristic of the הִפְעִיל pattern.

The first root letter י is replaced by the וֹ vowel in the הִפְעִיל pattern. Our textbook noted this variation in the case of the participle מוֹצִיא, appearing in the blessing over bread. Notice in the Grammar Enrichment chart that this same variation appears in all הִפְעִיל

forms of the roots יָדַע, יָצָא, and יָשַׁב, as well as the root הָלַךְ.

When the first root letter is א or ח or ע, the vowels under the prefix and the first root letter in the perfect forms will be הֶ◌ֱ◌ִי instead of הִ◌ְ◌ִי . The participle and imperfect forms will have the vowels ◌ַ◌ֲ◌ִי instead of ◌ַ◌ְ◌ִי .

Additional Reading and Translation Practice [pages 122–126]

1. שֶׁהֶחֱיָנוּ can be found in the gender-sensitive *Gates of Prayer* on page 178.

2. The song "Mah Navu" can be found in *Shireinu Songbook: A Songbook for Camps, Conclaves, Kallot and Retreats (2nd edition)* on page 41.

3. The קְדֻשָׁה can be found in the gender-sensitive *Gates of Prayer* on pages 116–117. The excerpt included in our textbook is on page 117.

4. The קִדּוּשׁ לֵיל שַׁבָּת can be found in the gender-sensitive *Gates of Prayer* on page 165.

5. הַבְדָּלָה can be found in the gender-sensitive *Gates of Prayer* on pages 172–175. The blessing included in our textbook is on page 174.

6. Genesis 1:4 can be found in *The Torah: A Modern Commentary*, revised edition, page 19.

7. מַעֲרִיב עֲרָבִים can be found in the gender-sensitive *Gates of Prayer* on page 50.

Exercises

Exercise 1 [page 128]

Translation	sg or pl	m or f	Form	Root	Verb
make remember, remind	sg	m	participle	ז־כ־ר	מַזְכִּיר
cause to eat, feed	sg	m	participle	א־כ־ל	מַאֲכִיל
cause to go out, bring out	sg	f	participle	י־צ־א	מוֹצִיאָה
make heard, proclaim	pl	m	participle	שׁ־מ־ע	מַשְׁמִיעִים
make remember, remind	pl	f	participle	ז־כ־ר	מַזְכִּירוֹת
will/may make ruler, crown	sg	m	imperfect	מ־ל־ך	יַמְלִיךְ
will/may bring up, raise	sg	m	imperfect	ע־ל־ה	יַעֲלֶה
will/may bring up, raise	sg	f	imperfect	ע־ל־ה	תַּעֲלֶה
will/may cause to eat, feed	sg	f	imperfect	א־כ־ל	תַּאֲכִיל
will/may make known	pl	m	imperfect	י־ד־ע	יוֹדִיעוּ
will/may make heard	pl	m	imperfect	שׁ־מ־ע	יַשְׁמִיעוּ
put to work, employed	sg	m	perfect	ע־ב־ד	הֶעֱבִיד
kept alive	sg	m	perfect	ח־י־ה	הֶחֱיָה
caused to go, led, brought	pl	m or f	perfect	ה־ל־ך	הוֹלִיכוּ
seated, caused to dwell	sg	f	perfect	י־שׁ־ב	הוֹשִׁיבָה

Tav Is for Torah – Book 4

Torah Study Text: Genesis 28:10–17 [pages 1–2]

Following are all the words, roots, endings, and prefixes appearing in Genesis 28:10–17 that have already been introduced. The book and chapter in which they were introduced is indicated in parentheses.

¹⁰וַיֵּצֵא יַעֲקֹב מִבְּאֵר שָׁבַע וַיֵּלֶךְ חָרָנָה: ¹¹וַיִּפְגַּע בַּמָּקוֹם וַיָּלֶן שָׁם כִּי־בָא הַשֶּׁמֶשׁ וַיִּקַּח מֵאַבְנֵי הַמָּקוֹם וַיָּשֶׂם מְרַאֲשֹׁתָיו וַיִּשְׁכַּב בַּמָּקוֹם הַהוּא: ¹²וַיַּחֲלֹם וְהִנֵּה סֻלָּם מֻצָּב אַרְצָה וְרֹאשׁוֹ מַגִּיעַ הַשָּׁמָיְמָה וְהִנֵּה מַלְאֲכֵי אֱלֹהִים עֹלִים וְיֹרְדִים בּוֹ: ¹³וְהִנֵּה יְהוָה נִצָּב עָלָיו וַיֹּאמַר אֲנִי יְהוָה אֱלֹהֵי אַבְרָהָם אָבִיךָ וֵאלֹהֵי יִצְחָק הָאָרֶץ אֲשֶׁר אַתָּה שֹׁכֵב עָלֶיהָ לְךָ אֶתְּנֶנָּה וּלְזַרְעֶךָ: ¹⁴וְהָיָה זַרְעֲךָ כַּעֲפַר הָאָרֶץ וּפָרַצְתָּ יָמָּה וָקֵדְמָה וְצָפֹנָה וָנֶגְבָּה וְנִבְרְכוּ בְךָ כָּל־מִשְׁפְּחֹת הָאֲדָמָה וּבְזַרְעֶךָ: ¹⁵וְהִנֵּה אָנֹכִי עִמָּךְ וּשְׁמַרְתִּיךָ בְּכֹל אֲשֶׁר־תֵּלֵךְ וַהֲשִׁבֹתִיךָ אֶל־הָאֲדָמָה הַזֹּאת כִּי לֹא אֶעֱזָבְךָ עַד אֲשֶׁר אִם־עָשִׂיתִי אֵת אֲשֶׁר־דִּבַּרְתִּי לָךְ: ¹⁶וַיִּיקַץ יַעֲקֹב מִשְּׁנָתוֹ וַיֹּאמֶר אָכֵן יֵשׁ יְהוָה בַּמָּקוֹם הַזֶּה וְאָנֹכִי לֹא יָדָעְתִּי: ¹⁷וַיִּירָא וַיֹּאמַר מַה־נּוֹרָא הַמָּקוֹם הַזֶּה אֵין זֶה כִּי אִם־בֵּית אֱלֹהִים וְזֶה שַׁעַר הַשָּׁמָיִם:

reversing vav, may also be translated as **and**:	— וְ
וַיֵּצֵא, וַיֵּלֶךְ, וַיִּפְגַּע, וַיָּלֶן, וַיִּקַּח, וַיָּשֶׂם, וַיִּשְׁכַּב, וַיַּחֲלֹם, וַיֹּאמַר, וְהָיָה, וּפָרַצְתָּ, וְנִבְרְכוּ, וּשְׁמַרְתִּיךָ, וַהֲשִׁבֹתִיךָ, וַיִּיקַץ, וַיִּירָא	
go out, come out (A.I.E. Ch 10), appears in the word וַיֵּצֵא	— י־צ־א

Jacob *(A.I.E. Ch 5)*	—	יַעֲקֹב
the *(attached prefix) (A.I.E. Ch 1)*, appears on the following words:	—	הַ־, הָ־

הַשֶּׁמֶשׁ, הַמָּקוֹם, הַהוּא, הַשָּׁמַיְמָה, הָאָרֶץ, הָאֲדָמָה,
הַזֹּאת, הַזֶּה, הַשָּׁמַיִם

from, than *(attached preposition) (A.I.E. Ch 10)*, appears on the following words:	—	מִ־, מֵי־

מִבְּאֵר שָׁבַע, מֵאַבְנֵי, מִשְׁנָתוֹ

walk, go *(B.I.F.B. Ch 9)*, appears in the word וַיֵּלֶךְ	—	ה־ל־ך
with, in *(attached preposition) (A.I.E. Ch 6)*, appears on the following words:	—	בְּ־

בַּמָּקוֹם, בּוֹ, בְּךָ, וּבְזַרְעֶךָ, בְּכֹל

place *m (B.I.F.B. Ch 7)*	—	מָקוֹם
there *(B.I.F.B. Ch 5)*	—	שָׁם
stone *f (B.I.F.B. Ch 5)*, appears in plural word-pair form: אַבְנֵי	—	אֶבֶן
his, him *(attached ending) m sg (A.I.E. Ch 9)*, appears on the following words:	—	־וֹ, ־יו

מֵרַאֲשֹׁתָיו, וְרֹאשׁוֹ, בּוֹ, עָלָיו, מִשְׁנָתוֹ

he, it *m (A.I.E. Ch 1)*	—	הוּא
behold, here [is]! *(B.I.F.B. Ch 9)*	—	הִנֵּה
and *(attached prefix) (A.I.E. Ch 2)*, appears on the following words:	—	וְ־, וּ־

וְהִנֵּה, וְרֹאשׁוֹ, וְיֹרְדִים, וֵאלֹהֵי, וּלְזַרְעֶךָ, וָקֵדְמָה, וְצָפֹנָה,
וָנֶגְבָּה, וּבְזַרְעֶךָ, וְאָנֹכִי, וְזֶה

earth, land *f (A.I.E. Ch 3)*, appears once with ending meaning toward *attached*	—	אֶרֶץ
head, top, beginning *m (B.I.F.B. Ch 5)*	—	רֹאשׁ
heavens, sky *m (A.I.E. Ch 3)*	—	שָׁמַיִם
angel, messenger *m (A.I.E. Ch 6)*, appears in plural word-pair form: מַלְאֲכֵי	—	מַלְאָךְ
God *m (A.I.E. Ch 4)*	—	אֱלֹהִים

go up, ascend *(B.I.F.B. Ch 9)*, appears in the participle עֹלִים —	עָ־ל־ה
plural ending (A.I.E. Ch 2), appears on the following words: עֹלִים, וְיֹרְדִים —	־ים
on, about *(A.I.E. Ch 8)* —	עַל
say, utter, tell *(B.I.F.B. Ch 1)*, appears in the following words: וַיֹּאמַר, וַיֹּאמֶר —	א־מ־ר
Abraham *(A.I.E. Ch 5)* —	אַבְרָהָם
father, ancestor *m (A.I.E. Ch 5)*, appears with pronoun ending: אָבִיךָ —	אָב
your, you *(attached ending) m sg (A.I.E. Ch 6)*, appears on the following words: — אָבִיךָ, לְךָ, וּלְזַרְעֶךָ, זַרְעֲךָ, בְּךָ, וּבְזַרְעֶךָ, עִמָּךְ, וּשְׁמַרְתִּיךָ, וַהֲשִׁבֹתִיךָ, אֶעֱזָבְךָ, לָךְ	־ךָ
Isaac *(A.I.E. Ch 5)* —	יִצְחָק
who, that, which *(A.I.E. Ch 8)* —	אֲשֶׁר
you *m sg (A.I.E. Ch 1)* —	אַתָּה
her, it *(attached ending) f sg (A.I.E. Ch 9)*, appears on the following words: עָלֶיהָ, אֶתְּנֶנָּה —	־הָ, ־יָה
to, for *(attached preposition) (A.I.E. Ch 8)*, appears on the following words: לְךָ, וּלְזַרְעֶךָ, לָךְ —	־ל
give, grant, permit *(A.I.E. Ch 4)*, appears in the word אֶתְּנֶנָּה —	נ־ת־ן
seed, offspring *m (B.I.F.B. Ch 7)* —	זֶרַע
be, exist *(B.I.F.B. Ch 1)*, appears in the word וְהָיָה —	ה־י־ה
like, as *(attached preposition) (A.I.E. Ch 7)*, appears on the word כַּעֲפַר —	־כ
bless *(A.I.E. Ch 1)*, appears in the word וְנִבְרְכוּ —	ב־ר־ך
all, every *(A.I.E. Ch 8)* —	כָּל, כֹּל
family *f (A.I.E. Ch 8)*, appears in plural form: מִשְׁפְּחֹת —	מִשְׁפָּחָה
earth, ground, land *f (A.I.E. Ch 8)* —	אֲדָמָה

with *(B.I.F.B. Ch 9)*, appears with pronoun ending: עִמְּךָ	—	עִם
guard, keep, preserve *(A.I.E. Ch 3)*, appears in the word וּשְׁמַרְתִּיךָ	—	שׁ־מ־ר
walk, go *(B.I.F.B. Ch 9)*, appears in the word תֵּלֵךְ	—	ה־ל־ך
to, toward *(B.I.F.B. Ch 3)*	—	אֶל
no, not *(B.I.F.B. Ch 3)*	—	לֹא
until, unto, as far as *(B.I.F.B. Ch 7)*	—	עַד
make, do, act *(A.I.E. Ch 7)*, appears in the word עָשִׂיתִי	—	ע־שׂ־ה
definite direct object marker (untranslatable) *(A.I.E. Ch 4)*	—	אֵת
speak, talk *(A.I.E. Ch 6)*, appears in the word דִּבַּרְתִּי	—	ד־ב־ר
know *(B.I.F.B. Ch 3)*, appears in the word יָדַעְתִּי	—	י־ד־ע
there is/are not, there is/are none *(A.I.E. Ch 7)*	—	אֵין
house m *(A.I.E. Ch 6)*, appears in word-pair form: בֵּית	—	בַּיִת

Translating the Torah Study Text [pages 2–4]

As your students work on their translations, the following comments may assist them:

1. The phrase בַּמָּקוֹם הַהוּא, "in that place," at the end of verse 11, does contain the pronoun הוּא, "he/it," with the prefix ה. This is a grammatical structure that will be explained in the Building Blocks section of this unit, in the next chapter.

2. In verse 12, the word אֶרֶץ, "earth/land," and the word הַשָּׁמַיִם, "the heavens/sky," both appear with a ה ending, as אַרְצָה and הַשָּׁמַיְמָה. This ה ending is explained in the Grammar Enrichment section of this unit, in the next chapter.

3. The word אֲשֶׁר, "that/who/which," can appear in combination with other words to express different meanings. In verse 15, it appears in the phrase עַד אֲשֶׁר אִם, all of which can be translated as *until*. In the same verse, it appears in the phrase אֵת אֲשֶׁר meaning "that which."

4. In verse 17, the word אֵין, "there is not/none," is used in combination with the word זֶה, "this" (a new vocabulary word in this chapter), to mean "this is not/none."

[pages 5–7]

It is often small details and ambiguities in the Hebrew language that give rise to both differences in translation and to midrash. You may wish to point out some of the following examples to your students, in addition to the details that give rise to the commentaries cited in this chapter's Torah Commentary section:

1. In verse 11, did Jacob use one or several stones as his pillow? (A well-known midrash, cited by Rashi on this verse, states that Jacob put several stones under his head, which were then fused by God into one, as indicated in verse 18.)

2. Notice that, in verse 14, when Jacob is told that his offspring will spread out over the earth, the directions are given in relation to the Land of Israel. The Hebrew does not literally state "to the west…east…north…and south" as three of our translations render it, but "to the Sea, to the east, to the north, to the Negev," as only Everett Fox's translation states.

3. In verse 14, we encounter the same phrase that appeared in Genesis 12:3, when God first spoke to Abraham, וְנִבְרְכוּ בְךָ כֹּל מִשְׁפְּחֹת הָאֲדָמָה, with one additional word added, וּבְזַרְעֶךָ. In the commentary by Richard Elliot Friedman, cited in *Bet Is for B'reishit*, Chapter 7, various interpretations of the meaning of the verb וְנִבְרְכוּ are explored. Notice that our four translations reflect different understandings of the meaning of this verb, and hence of this phrase:

    JPS: "All the families of the earth **shall bless themselves by you** and your descendants"

    ArtScroll *Chumash*: "all the families of the earth **shall bless themselves by you** and by your offspring"

    Everett Fox: "All the clans of the soil **will find blessing through you** and through your seed"

    Jerusalem Bible: "**and in thee** and in thy seed **shall** all the families of the earth **be blessed**"

4. When Jacob awakens from his dream, he states (in verse 16) וְאָנֹכִי לֹא יָדָעְתִּי, "and I knew not."

    Three of our translations add the word "it": "and I did not know it" or "and I knew it not." Only the ArtScroll *Chumash* leaves the translation as the literal Hebrew: "and I did not know." Jacob's awareness is limited by the addition of the word "it" to the realization that "God is in this place."

Without including the word "it," Jacob's statement "I did not know" is much more open: there can be all sorts of things, aside from the realization that God is in this place, that he did not know.

Vocabulary [page 7]

All the new vocabulary words are identified and highlighted within the Torah Study Text at the beginning of Chapter 2, on page 15.

The word יָם, "sea," appears with the ה ending meaning "toward" (to be introduced in the Grammar Enrichment section of Chapter 2).

The Hebrew Root [pages 8–9]

The root יָרֵא follows the פָּעַל pattern with some irregularities that are caused both by its root letters א and י and by the fact that it is a type of verb known as a stative verb, a verb that indicates a state of being as opposed to an action or motion. The participle form for the root יָרֵא is actually the regular participle form for stative verbs: ◻◻◻וֹת, ◻◻◻ים, ◻◻◻ָה, ◻◻◻.

The word וַיִּירָא, "and he was afraid/awestruck," in verse 17 is a הוא imperfect form with a reversing *vav* attached. The word נוֹרָא, "awesome/fearsome," in verse 17 is an adjective derived from this root.

The root לָקַח in the פָּעַל pattern is almost completely regular in the perfect and participle forms, except for the usual slight variations caused by the final root letter ח. In the imperfect, it is irregular, with the first letter ל disappearing in all the forms.

The word וַיִּקַּח, "and he took," in verse 11 is a הוא imperfect form with a reversing *vav* attached.

Exercises

Exercise 2 [page 11]

2. Draw a line connecting each Hebrew word to its English translation. For some
   words, there can be more than one correct translation.

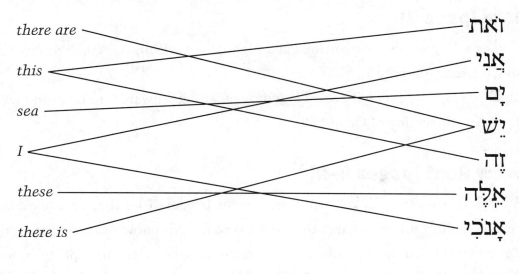

there are

this

sea

I

these

there is

זֹאת

אֲנִי

יָם

יֵשׁ

זֶה

אֵלֶּה

אָנֹכִי

Exercise 3 [page 12]

3. The following are plural forms of words introduced as vocabulary in this chapter.
   Draw a line connecting each plural word to its singular form or forms. Translate
   both into English.

we _____

these _____

seas _____

אֲנַחְנוּ

אֵלֶּה

יָמִים

זֶה   this _____

זֹאת   this _____

יָם   sea _____

אֲנִי   I _____

אָנֹכִי   I _____

Exercise 4 [page 12]

a. the great sea

   [the] wind of the sea

   [the] waters of the sea

   from sea unto/until/as far as sea

   the sea of Egypt

b. I am your *(m sg)* son.

   I am your *(m pl)* God.

   I am the king.

   This is the king.

   This is the Torah. (*This phrase appears in the Torah service, as the scroll is lifted following the Torah reading. It can be found in the gender-sensitive GOP on page 145.*)

c. This is the sea.

   This is the people.

   This is the place.

   This is the prophet.

   This is the angel/messenger.

d. all this

   all these

   Who are these?

   Who is this *(f)*?

   This is the woman/wife.

e. There is a God.

   There is a healer/one who heals.

   There is healing.

   There is compassion/mercy.

   There is a way.

f. Who am I?

   I am a lad/youth/young man.

   I am with you *(m pl)*.

   I am the God of your *(m sg)* father

   Am I the guard/keeper of my brother? (Am I my brother's keeper? *Cain's question to God after killing his brother Abel in Genesis 4:9.*)

Exercise 5 [page 13]

Translation	Form	Root	Verb
he/it will/shall/may be or let … be	imperfect	ה־י־ה	יִהְיֶה
he/it worked/served or was …ing/did …/had	perfect	ע־ב־ד	עָבַד
sit/settle/dwell m pl	participle	י־שׁ־ב	יוֹשְׁבִים
take m pl	participle	ל־ק־ח	לוֹקְחִים
he/it took or was …ing/did …/has taken/had …	perfect	ל־ק־ח	לָקַח
bless m sg	participle	ב־ר־ך	מְבָרֵךְ
make ruler/crown m sg	participle	מ־ל־ך	מַמְלִיךְ
take out/bring out m sg	participle	י־צ־א	מוֹצִיא
she/it went or was …ing/did …/has gone/had …	perfect	ה־ל־ך	הָלְכָה
she/it feared/was in awe of	perfect	י־ר־א	יָרְאָה
know f pl	participle	י־ד־ע	יוֹדְעוֹת
she/it will/shall/may build or let her build	imperfect	ב־נ־ה	תִּבְנֶה

Notes on

Torah Study Text: Vocabulary and Root Review [page 15]

Vocabulary words that appear in our Torah Study Text in variant forms or with prefixes or suffixes attached were noted in the Vocabulary section of the previous chapter of this Teacher's Guide. The various forms of the new roots ל־ק־ח and י־ר־א were explained in the Hebrew Root section of the previous chapter of this Teacher's Guide.

Building Blocks

זֶה and זֹאת and אֵלֶה [pages 16–17]

Following is a slightly more technical explanation of the words זֶה, זֹאת, and אֵלֶה that you may wish to offer your students if they are grammatically inclined.

The words זֶה, זֹאת, and אֵלֶה are known as "demonstratives." In both Hebrew and English, there are two different ways that demonstratives are used: as pronouns and as adjectives.

In the first examples presented in the textbook, the words זֶה, זֹאת, and אֵלֶה are all used as demonstrative pronouns, which means that they take the place of a pronoun in the sentence. For example, in the sentence זֶה הָאִישׁ, "This is the man," the word זֶה is in the place of the pronoun הוּא, "he/it": הוּא הָאִישׁ, "He/It is the man."

In the second set of examples presented in the textbook, the use of demonstratives as pronouns is contrasted with their use as adjectives. When demonstratives are used as adjectives, they do not replace a pronoun in a sentence. Instead, they act as an adjective, describing a noun. As was explained in Chapter 5 of *Aleph Isn't Enough*, in Hebrew, adjectives come after the noun they describe and must agree with the noun they describe in number (singular versus plural), gender (masculine versus feminine), and definiteness. Since any noun described as "this" or "these" would, by definition, be a definite noun ("**this** noun" as opposed to "**a** noun"), the nouns that are described by the demonstrative adjectives זֶה, זֹאת, and אֵלֶה generally (though not always) have the definite article ה attached. The demonstrative adjectives must then also have the definite article ה attached.

This and That [page 17]

The pronouns הִיא, "she," הֵם, "they," *(m)*, and הֵן, "they," *(f)*, have not been formally presented as vocabulary, though they appeared in *Aleph Isn't Enough* in the Grammar Enrichment charts of Chapters 1 and 9. You may wish to refer back to those charts.

All the examples provided in the textbook use the subject pronouns as demonstrative adjectives. The subject pronouns can be used as demonstrative pronouns as well, though it is an act of interpretation on the part of the translator to decide whether, for example, הוּא הָאִישׁ would mean "He is the man" or "That is the man."

Additional Reading and Translation Practice [pages 20–23]

1. שֶׁהֶחֱיָנוּ can be found in the gender-sensitive *Gates of Prayer* on page 178.

2. The Passover Four Questions can be found in *The Open Door Hagaddah* on page 30.

3. וְזֹאת הַתּוֹרָה can be found in the gender-sensitive *Gates of Prayer* on page 145.

4. וְנֶאֱמַר can be found in the gender-sensitive *Gates of Prayer* on page 149. The word נֶאֱמַר is a נִפְעַל form from the root א־מ־ר. This form will be introduced in Chapter 10 on pages 130–131.

5. From Deuteronomy 1:1—The word עֲרָבָה means "desert," "plain," or "steppe." It is also used as a name for the arid steppe adjacent to the Jordan River, the desert area near the Dead Sea.

6. The evening version of מִי כָמֹכָה can be found in the gender-sensitive *Gates of Prayer* on page 53.

7. The Blessing after the Haftarah can be found in the gender-sensitive *Gates of Prayer* on page 145.

Exercises

Exercise 1 [pages 23–24]

a. This is the house.

   This is the mezuzah/doorpost.

   These are the seeds/offspring.

   These are your *(m sg)* seeds/offspring.

   These are their brothers.

b. This is his heart.

   This is his soul/mind/breath.

   These are the faces.

These are the hands.

This is her/its head.

c. this way/road/path

that way/road/path

these ways/roads/paths

those ways/roads/paths

those words/things

d. this angel/messenger

that angel/messenger

those angels/messengers

These are the angels/messengers.

This is the angel/messenger.

e. the great sea

in the great sea

this sea

that sea

in this great sea

f. This is the tree.

These are the trees.

this tree

that tree

these trees

Exercise 2 [page 24]

2. In each of the following phrases or sentences, circle the one form in the parentheses that is grammatically correct. Translate.

a. הָעַיִן (הָאֵלֶּה, זֶה, (הַזֹּאת))   this eye _____

b. הַפָּנִים (הַזֶּה, (הָאֵלֶּה), זֶה)   this face *or* these faces _____

c. ((זֹאת), הָאֵלֶּה, הָהֵם) לֹא הַדֶּרֶךְ.   This is not the way. _____

d. ((זֶה), הַהוּא, אֵלֶּה) רֵעֲךָ.   This is your (*m sg*) friend/companion/fellow/ _____ neighbor. _____

e. אָנֹכִי הָאָדָם (הַזֹּאת, זֶה, (הַהוּא)).   I am that man. _____

f. אֲנִי מֵהָאֲדָמָה ((הַזֹּאת), זֶה, הַהֵם).   I am from this earth. _____

g. מִי הַחוֹלִים ((הָהֵם), הַזֶּה, זֹאת)?   Who are those sick [people]? _____

h. יֵשׁ צֶדֶק בָּעִיר (זֶה, (הַזֹּאת), אֵלֶּה).   There is righteousness/justice in _____ this city. _____

i. אֵין שָׁלוֹם בָּאֶרֶץ (הָאֵלֶּה, הָהֵם, (הַהִיא)).   There is no peace in _____ that land. _____

j. ((הַזֹּאת), זֶה, אֵלֶּה) דַּם אָבִינוּ.   This is the blood of our father. _____

From Our Texts: *Mishnah Pe-ah* 1:1 [page 27]

You may wish to compare this passage with the variation that appears in the morning liturgy. In the Reform liturgy, the line referring to *pe-ah, bikurim,* and *re'ayon* has been omitted, though it is preserved in the traditional liturgy. (See page 105 in the gender-sensitive *Gates of Prayer.*)

The variation on the second half of this passage (beginning with the words אָב וָאֵם כָּבוֹד, "honoring father and mother," and expanding the list of mitzvot enumerated) that appears in the morning liturgy comes from the Talmud, *Shabbat* 127a.

Torah Study Text: Exodus 3:1–7 [page 28]

Following are all the words, roots, endings, and prefixes appearing in Exodus 3:1–7 that have already been introduced. The book and chapter in which they were introduced is indicated in parentheses.

¹וּמֹשֶׁה הָיָה רֹעֶה אֶת־צֹאן יִתְרוֹ חֹתְנוֹ כֹּהֵן מִדְיָן וַיִּנְהַג אֶת־הַצֹּאן אַחַר הַמִּדְבָּר וַיָּבֹא אֶל־הַר הָאֱלֹהִים חֹרֵבָה: ²וַיֵּרָא מַלְאַךְ יְהֹוָה אֵלָיו בְּלַבַּת־אֵשׁ מִתּוֹךְ הַסְּנֶה וַיַּרְא וְהִנֵּה הַסְּנֶה בֹּעֵר בָּאֵשׁ וְהַסְּנֶה אֵינֶנּוּ אֻכָּל: ³וַיֹּאמֶר מֹשֶׁה אָסֻרָה־נָּא וְאֶרְאֶה אֶת־הַמַּרְאֶה הַגָּדֹל הַזֶּה מַדּוּעַ לֹא־יִבְעַר הַסְּנֶה: ⁴וַיַּרְא יְהֹוָה כִּי סָר לִרְאוֹת וַיִּקְרָא אֵלָיו אֱלֹהִים מִתּוֹךְ הַסְּנֶה וַיֹּאמֶר מֹשֶׁה מֹשֶׁה וַיֹּאמֶר הִנֵּנִי: ⁵וַיֹּאמֶר אַל־תִּקְרַב הֲלֹם שַׁל־נְעָלֶיךָ מֵעַל רַגְלֶיךָ כִּי הַמָּקוֹם אֲשֶׁר אַתָּה עוֹמֵד עָלָיו אַדְמַת־קֹדֶשׁ הוּא: ⁶וַיֹּאמֶר אָנֹכִי אֱלֹהֵי אָבִיךָ אֱלֹהֵי אַבְרָהָם אֱלֹהֵי יִצְחָק וֵאלֹהֵי יַעֲקֹב וַיַּסְתֵּר מֹשֶׁה פָּנָיו כִּי יָרֵא מֵהַבִּיט אֶל־הָאֱלֹהִים: ⁷וַיֹּאמֶר יְהֹוָה רָאֹה רָאִיתִי אֶת־עֳנִי עַמִּי אֲשֶׁר בְּמִצְרָיִם וְאֶת־צַעֲקָתָם שָׁמַעְתִּי מִפְּנֵי נֹגְשָׂיו כִּי יָדַעְתִּי אֶת־מַכְאֹבָיו:

Moses *(A.I.E. Ch 4)*	—	מֹשֶׁה
and *(attached prefix) (A.I.E. Ch 2)*, appears on the following words:	—	וְ־, וּ־

וּמֹשֶׁה, וְהִנֵּה, וְהַסְּנֶה, וְאֶרְאֶה, וֵאלֹהֵי, וְאֶת

be, exist *(B.I.F.B. Ch 1)*, appears in the word הָיָה	—	ה־י־ה
definite direct object marker (untranslatable) *(A.I.E. Ch 4)*, appears five times	—	אֶת

his, him *(attached ending) m sg (A.I.E. Ch 9)*, *appears on the*
following words: — ‫וֹ־, ־יו‬

‫חֹתְנוֹ, אֵלָיו, עָלָיו, פָּנָיו, נֹגְשָׂיו, מַכְאֹבָיו‬

reversing vav, *may also be translated*
as and: — ‫וַ־‬

‫וַיִּנְהַג, וַיָּבֹא, וַיֵּרָא, וַיַּרְא, וַיֹּאמֶר, וַיִּקְרָא, וַיַּסְתֵּר‬

the *(attached prefix) (A.I.E. Ch 1)*, *appears on the*
following words: — ‫הַ־, הָ־‬

‫הַצֹּאן, הַמִּדְבָּר, הָאֱלֹהִים, הַסְּנֶה, הַמַּרְאֶה, הַגָּדֹל, הַזֶּה, הַמָּקוֹם‬

come *(T.I.F.T. Ch 3)*, *appears in*
the word ‫וַיָּבֹא‬ — ‫ב־ו־א‬

to, toward *(B.I.F.B. Ch 3)* — ‫אֶל‬

mountain, mount *m (B.I.F.B. Ch 9)* — ‫הַר‬

God *m (A.I.E. Ch 4)* — ‫אֱלֹהִים‬

angel, messenger *m (A.I.E. Ch 6)* — ‫מַלְאַךְ‬

with, in *(attached preposition) (A.I.E. Ch 6)*, *appears on the*
following words: — ‫בְּ־‬

‫בְּלַבַּת, בָּאֵשׁ, בְּמִצְרַיִם‬

from, than *(attached preposition) (A.I.E. Ch 10)*, *appears on the*
following words: — ‫מ־, מֵי־‬

‫מִתּוֹךְ, מֵעַל, מֵהַבִּיט‬

behold, here [is]! *(B.I.F.B. Ch 9)* — ‫הִנֵּה‬

eat, consume *(A.I.E. Ch 2)*, *appears in the*
word ‫אֶכָל‬ — ‫א־כ־ל‬

say, utter, tell *(B.I.F.B. Ch 1)*, *appears in the*
word ‫וַיֹּאמֶר‬ — ‫א־מ־ר‬

big, great *adj (A.I.E. Ch 5)* — ‫גָּדוֹל‬

this *m (T.I.F.T. Ch 1)* — ‫זֶה‬

no, not *(B.I.F.B. Ch 3)* — ‫לֹא‬

to, for *(attached preposition) (A.I.E. Ch 8)*, *appears on*
the word ‫לִרְאוֹת‬ — ‫לְ־‬

your, you *(attached ending) m sg (A.I.E. Ch 6)*, *appears on*
the following words: — ‫ךָ‬

‫נַעֲלֶיךָ, רַגְלֶיךָ, אָבִיךָ‬

on, about *(A.I.E. Ch 8)*	—	עַל
place *m (B.I.F.B. Ch 7)*	—	מָקוֹם
who, that, which *(A.I.E. Ch 8)*	—	אֲשֶׁר
you *m sg (A.I.E. Ch 1)*	—	אַתָּה
earth, ground, land *f (A.I.E. Ch 8), appears in word-pair form:* אַדְמַת	—	אֲדָמָה
holiness, sanctity *m (A.I.E. Ch 7)*	—	קֹדֶשׁ
he, it *m (A.I.E. Ch 1)*	—	הוּא
I *(T.I.F.T. Ch 1)*	—	אָנֹכִי
father, ancestor *m (A.I.E. Ch 5), appears with pronoun ending:* אָבִיךָ	—	אָב
Abraham *(A.I.E. Ch 5)*	—	אַבְרָהָם
Isaac *(A.I.E. Ch 5)*	—	יִצְחָק
Jacob *(A.I.E. Ch 5)*	—	יַעֲקֹב
face *m pl and f pl (B.I.F.B. Ch 1), appears with pronoun ending:* פָּנָיו	—	פָּנִים
people, nation *m (A.I.E. Ch 4), appears with pronoun ending:* עַמִּי	—	עַם
Egypt *(A.I.E. Ch 10)*	—	מִצְרַיִם
their *(attached ending) (B.I.F.B. Ch 5), appears on the word* צַעֲקָתָם	—	ָם
hear, listen, obey *(A.I.E. Ch 1), appears in the word* שָׁמַעְתִּי	—	שׁ־מ־ע
know *(B.I.F.B. Ch 3), appears in the word* יָדַעְתִּי	—	י־ד־ע

Translating the Torah Study Text [pages 29–31]

As your students work on their translations, the following comments may assist them:

1. In verse 1, אַחַר הַמִּדְבָּר, "behind the wilderness," is an awkward phrase. Of our four Torah translations, only Everett Fox translates it that way. The other three alter the wording slightly: "into the wilderness" (JPS), "far into the wilderness" (the ArtScroll *Chumash*), and "far away into the desert" (the *Jerusalem Bible*).

2. Notice that the word חֹרֵבָה, "toward Horeb," has the ה ending meaning "toward," introduced in the last chapter.

3. In the first unit of *Bet Is for B'reishit*, Chapter 2, we explained that there is no past or future tense in classical Hebrew. Perfect verbs describe action that has been completed, and imperfect verbs describe action that is ongoing or incomplete. Often, but not always, completed action is in the past, and incomplete or ongoing action projects forward into the future. In this Torah Study Text, however, we have in verse 3 an example of an imperfect verb expressing incomplete action in the present: מַדּוּעַ לֹא־יִבְעַר הַסְּנֶה, "why doesn't the bush burn up/why isn't the bush burning up?" (The ArtScroll *Chumash* is the only one of our translations to render this in the future: "why will the bush not be burned?") We also find, in verse 7, an example of a perfect verb that could be understood as expressing completed action in the present: יָדַעְתִּי אֶת־מַכְאֹבָיו. "I know/have known its sufferings." Two of our translations render this perfect verb in the past tense and two in the present.

4. In Hebrew, there cannot be a dangling preposition. If a preposition occurs at the end of a sentence or a phrase, it will have a pronoun ending attached. For example, in verse 5, it says, הַמָּקוֹם אֲשֶׁר אַתָּה עוֹמֵד עָלָיו, "the place that you are standing on **it**," because it cannot simply say, הַמָּקוֹם אֲשֶׁר אַתָּה עוֹמֵד עַל, "the place that you are standing on." Dangling prepositions are also not regarded as good form in English, which is why all of our translations reword this phrase in English to read "the place on [*or:* upon] which you stand [*or:* thou dost stand]."

 **[pages 31–33]**

The last verse of our Torah Study Text, verse 7, contains several details that highlight the different orientations of our four translations:

1. The opening words וַיֹּאמֶר יְהֹוָה, "And the Eternal said," are translated in the most idiomatic way in the JPS version, with the verb itself changed: "And the LORD continued." They are translated most literally by the ArtScroll *Chumash* ("HASHEM said") and

TAV IS FOR TORAH • CHAPTER 3

by the *Jerusalem Bible* ("And the LORD said"). Everett Fox provides a different way of rendering the reversing *vav:* "Now YHWH said." (Notice also the different names for God, discussed earlier in this Teacher's Guide, in the notes to Chapter 3 of *Bet Is for B'reishit*.)

2. The use of the infinitive absolute רָאֹה with the verb רָאִיתִי, "I have seen," indicates emphasis. (See note on these forms in the Hebrew Root section below.) The most idiomatic translation is, again, the JPS version, with the verb again changed: "I have marked well." The ArtScroll *Chumash* and the *Jerusalem Bible* both try to indicate the emphasis in the Hebrew by inserting an emphatic term in the English: "I have **indeed** seen" and "I have **surely** seen." Everett Fox tries to render the repetitive feel of the Hebrew in his translation, with the poetic and very literal translation "I have seen, yes, seen."

3. In the continuation of the verse, there is a switch in the Hebrew from the plural pronoun ending on the word צַעֲקָתָם, "their cry," to the singular pronoun endings on the words נֹגְשָׂיו, "its taskmasters," and מַכְאֹבָיו, "its sufferings." The singular pronoun endings refer back to the singular Hebrew word עַמִּי, "my nation/my people." None of our four translations mix up the plural and singular pronouns in the English. What is interesting, however, is that three of our translations render all the pronouns as "their," while the ArtScroll *Chumash* renders all the pronouns as "its": "I have indeed seen the affliction of My people that is in Egypt and I have heard **its** outcry because of **its** taskmasters, for I have known of **its** sufferings." The use of this pronoun serves to reinforce the collective identity and collective fate of the people as a single entity.

Vocabulary [page 33]

All the new vocabulary words are identified and highlighted within the Torah Study Text at the beginning of Chapter 4, on page 41.

1. כֹּהֵן, "priest," is a common Jewish last name: Cohen. Most, though not all, of the Jews with this last name are descendants of the ancient priests.

2. The word אַחַר, "after/behind," is used both temporally (in relation to time) and spatially (in relation to space, physical location).

3. The word מִדְבָּר, "wilderness/desert," appears once with the prefix הַ attached. The Hebrew name for the fourth book of the Torah (Numbers) is בְּמִדְבָּר, "in the wilderness."

4. The word אֵשׁ, "fire," appears in a word pair בְּלַבַּת־אֵשׁ and with the prefix בְּ attached.

5. The word תּוֹךְ only appears in this passage with the prefix מ attached.

6. The word כִּי can mean "because/for," as it does in verses 5, 6, and 7, or it can mean "that," as in verse 4. Your students have now seen several different Hebrew words that can be translated into English as "that," all used differently. Some students appreciate a fuller explanation of the usage of all these words for "that":

a. The word כִּי, whether it means "because" "for" or "that," is a type of conjunction, linking two separate parts of a sentence:

(verse 6)

| **Moses hid his face _because, for_ he was afraid** | — | וַיַּסְתֵּר מֹשֶׁה פָּנָיו כִּי יָרֵא |

(verse 4)

| **The Eternal saw _that_ he had turned aside** | — | וַיַּרְא יְהוָֹה כִּי סָר |

b. The word אֲשֶׁר, which can be translated as "that," "who," or "which," introduces a subordinate clause within a sentence:

| **I have seen the affliction of my people _that_ are in Egypt** | — | רָאִיתִי אֶת־עֳנִי עַמִּי אֲשֶׁר בְּמִצְרָיִם |

c. The word הַהוּא is a demonstrative adjective:

| **on _that_ day** | — | בַּיּוֹם הַהוּא |

The Hebrew Root [pages 34–36]

In verbs forms of the root ר־א־ה, the same irregularities occur as in other verbs with the final root letter ה. In a few forms, there are slight variations in vowels due to the middle root letter א.

The word וַיֵּרָא, "appeared," in verse 2 is a form of the root ר־א־ה, in a verb pattern that has not been introduced: the נִפְעַל pattern. In this pattern, the root ר־א־ה means "be seen" or "appear." Though the root is in an unfamiliar pattern, it is still possible to note that it is an imperfect הוּא form with a reversing _vav_ attached. The final root letter ה often drops out when the reversing _vav_ is attached (as in the word וַיְהִי, "and it was").

The word וַיַּרְא, "[he] saw," in verses 2 and 4 is a הוּא imperfect form with reversing _vav_ attached. The final root letter ה has dropped out with the reversing vav attached.

The word וְאֶרְאֶה, "and I will see," in verse 3, is a פָּעַל imperfect אֲנִי form.

The word מַרְאֶה, "sight," in verse 3 is a noun derived from this root.

The word לִרְאוֹת, "to see," in verse 4, is one type of Hebrew פָּעַל infinitive form, called the infinitive construct. This is the type of infinitive that can have prefixes, such as the ל, meaning "to," attached. The final root letter ה is replaced with וֹת in infinitive construct forms.

The word רָאֹה in verse 7 is the other type of Hebrew infinitive, called the infinitive absolute. This infinitive form is most often used in the way in which it appears in this verse, alongside another form of the verb as an intensification or emphasis of that verb. In this case, it appears with רָאִיתִי, the פָּעַל perfect אֲנִי form of ר-א-ה.

Hebrew roots such as ב-ו-א are characterized by their middle root letter ו, which drops out in many verb forms.

The word וַיָּבֹא, "and he came," in verse 1, is a פָּעַל imperfect הוּא form with reversing *vav* attached.

Exercises

Exercise 2 [page 38]

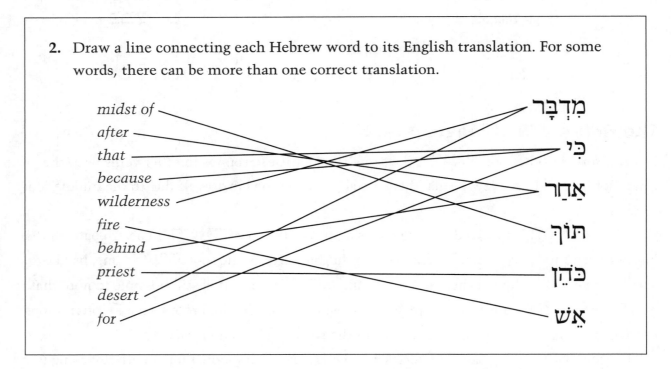

2. Draw a line connecting each Hebrew word to its English translation. For some words, there can be more than one correct translation.

midst of
after
that
because
wilderness
fire
behind
priest
desert
for

מִדְבָּר
כִּי
אַחַר
תּוֹךְ
כֹּהֵן
אֵשׁ

Exercise 3 [page 38]

3. The following are plural forms of words introduced as vocabulary in this chapter. Draw a line connecting each plural word to its singular form. Translate both into English.

deserts, wilderness	מִדְבָּרוֹת	מִדְבָּר	desert, wilderness
fires	אֵשִׁים		
deserts, wilderness	מִדְבָּרִים	כֹּהֵן	priest
priests	כֹּהֲנִים	אֵשׁ	fire

Exercise 4 [pages 38–39]

a. the great priest (*i.e.*, the High Priest)

   a priest and a prophet

   in the hand of the priest *or* with (i.e., by) the hand of the priest

   the eyes of the priest

   their priests

b. in the wilderness/desert

   the way/path/road of the wilderness

   a wilderness/desert of mountains

   the wilderness/desert of Egypt

   the wilderness/desert of the peoples/nations

c. after/behind this

   after this word/thing

   after the Sabbath

   after/behind the wind

   after/behind his brothers

d. blood and fire

   in the fire and in the water

   the fire of God

   light of fire

   stones of fire

e. in his/its midst, within him/it

in her/its midst, within her/it

in our midst, within us

from the midst of/out of/from among you *(m pl)*

in their midst, within them

Exercise 5 [page 39]

Translation	Form	Root	Verb
they heard/listened *or* were …ing/did …/had …/have …	perfect	שׁ־מ־ע	שָׁמְעוּ
they were/have been/had been	perfect	ה־י־ה	הָיוּ
they went up/ascended *or* did …/were …ing/had …	perfect	ע־ל־ה	עָלוּ
he took/did take/was taking/had taken/has taken	perfect	ל־ק־ח	לָקַח
he saw/did see/was seeing/had seen/has seen	perfect	ר־א־ה	רָאָה
they saw/did see/were seeing/had seen/have seen	perfect	ר־א־ה	רָאוּ
see *m pl*	participle	ר־א־ה	רוֹאִים
they came/did …/were …ing/have come/had come	perfect	ב־ו־א	בָּאוּ
he will/shall/may come *or* let him come	imperfect	ב־ו־א	יָבוֹא
she will/shall/may come *or* let her come	imperfect	ב־ו־א	תָּבוֹא
she will/shall/may praise *or* let her praise	imperfect	ה־ל־ל	תְּהַלֵּל
they will/shall/may say/tell *or* let them say/tell	imperfect	א־מ־ר	יֹאמְרוּ

Notes on

Torah Study Text: Vocabulary and Root Review [page 41]

Vocabulary words that appear in our Torah Study Text in variant forms or with prefixes or suffixes attached were noted in the Vocabulary section of the previous chapter of this Teacher's Guide. The various forms of the new roots ר־א־ה and ב־ו־א were explained in the Hebrew Root section of the previous chapter of this Teacher's Guide.

Building Blocks

Perfect Forms [page 42]

The regular perfect אֲנִי or אָנֹכִי ending is תִי. The תִי ending is a variation that occurs when the final root letter is א or ה.

The regular פָּעַל perfect form is תִי ▢▢▢.

The regular פָּעֵל perfect form is תִי ▢▢▢.

The regular הִפְעִיל perfect form is תִי ▢▢▢הֶ. The example הֶאֱמַנְתִּי, "I trusted/believed," actually contains a slight variation in the vowels caused by the first root letter א.

Imperfect Forms [page 42]

There are many variations in the vowels of imperfect forms, caused by various root letters.

The regular פָּעַל imperfect form is: אֶ▢▢▢, but most of the verb roots introduced thus far do not follow this regular pattern, but contain some variation in vowels due to root letters ה, א, ע, ח, or י or ו.

The regular פָּעֵל imperfect form is אֲ▢▢▢.

The regular הִפְעִיל imperfect form is אַ▢▢י▢. The example אַאֲמִין, "I will/may trust/believe," contains a slight variation in the vowels caused by the first root letter א.

Torah Study Text with Building Blocks [page 44]

The word רָאִיתִי, "I have seen," comes from the new root ר־א־ה. The final root letter ה drops out in perfect אֲנִי forms.

[pages 45–46]

You may wish to point out to your students that the imperfect forms of the root הָ-לַ-ךְ in both the פָּעַל and הִפְעִיל patterns are like those verbs with the first root letter יֹ. It also may be helpful to note that, in the הִפְעִיל pattern, verbs with first root letter יֹ have a vowel וֹ in place of the consonant יֹ.

Additional Reading and Translation Practice [pages 46–50]

1. Psalm 23 is included in the memorial service in *Gates of Prayer: The New Union Prayerbook* on page 546.

2. The song כִּי אֶשְׁמְרָה שַׁבָּת appears in the gender-sensitive *Gates of Prayer* on page 160.

3. Psalm 121 is included in the memorial service in the *Gates of Prayer: The New Union Prayerbook* on pages 546–547.

4. Isaiah 12:2 is included at the opening of the *Havdalah* service in the gender-sensitive *Gates of Prayer* on page 172.

5. אֲדוֹן עוֹלָם appears in the gender-sensitive *Gates of Prayer* on page 156.

Exercises

Exercise 1 [page 51]

a. my heart
   in my heart
   in our heart
   with all your *(m sg)* heart
   my heart

b. my lord
   our lord
   my lords *(also: Adonai, a name for God used in place of the four-letter unpronounceable name of God)*
   our lords
   your *(m pl)* lords

c. righteousness/justice and kindness
   his righteousness/justice

my righteousness/justice

your (m sg) righteousnesses/justice

my righteousnesses/justice

d. breath of life

breath/soul of man/humanity

my breath/soul

my breaths

their breaths/souls

e. great compassion/mercy

kindness and compassion/mercy

his compassion/mercy

my compassion/mercy

in/with my great compassion/mercy

f. my strength/valor/might

your (m sg) strength/valor/might

her strength/valor/might

my strengths or my [acts of] strength/valor/might

the strengths of my people or the [acts of] strength/valor/might of my people

Exercise 2 [pages 51–52]

Translation	Form	Root	Verb
I will/shall/may come or let me come	imperfect	ב־ו־א	אָבוֹא
I chose/did choose/was …ing/had …/have …	perfect	ב־ח־ר	בָּחַרְתִּי
I worked/served or did …/was …ing/had …	perfect	ע־ב־ד	עָבַדְתִּי
I will/shall/may build or let me build	imperfect	ב־נ־ה	אֶבְנֶה
I will/shall/may be or let me be	imperfect	ה־י־ה	אֶהְיֶה
I will/shall/may bless or let me bless	imperfect	ב־ר־ך	אֲבָרֵךְ
I ruled/reigned or did …/was …ing/had …/have …	perfect	מ־ל־ך	מָלַכְתִּי
I guarded/kept or did …/was …ing/had …/have …	perfect	ש־מ־ר	שָׁמַרְתִּי

I knew/did know/had known/have known	perfect	יָ־דָ־ע	יָדַעְתִּי
I feared/was in awe of *or* did …/was …ing/had …	perfect	יָ־רָ־א	יָרֵאתִי
I will/shall/may see *or* let me see	imperfect	רָ־אָ־ה	אֶרְאֶה
I will/shall/may praise *or* let me praise	imperfect	הָ־לָ־ל	אֲהַלֵּל
I sanctified/did …/was …/had …/have …	perfect	קָ־דָ־שׁ	קִדַּשְׁתִּי
I did/made *or* I did …/was …ing/had …/have …	perfect	עָ־שָׂ־ה	עָשִׂיתִי
I will/shall/may bring out *or* let me bring out	imperfect	יָ־צָ־א	אוֹצִיא
I brought out/did …/was …/had …/have …	perfect	יָ־צָ־א	הוֹצֵאתִי

Notes on

Torah Study Text: Leviticus 19:1–4, 15–17, 33–34 [page 57]

Following are all the words, roots, endings, and prefixes appearing in Leviticus 19:1–4, 15–17, 33–34 that have already been introduced. The book and chapter in which they were introduced is indicated in parentheses.

Leviticus 19:1–4

¹וַיְדַבֵּ֥ר יְהֹוָ֖ה אֶל־מֹשֶׁ֥ה לֵּאמֹֽר: ²דַּבֵּ֞ר אֶל־כָּל־עֲדַ֧ת בְּנֵֽי־יִשְׂרָאֵ֛ל וְאָמַרְתָּ֥ אֲלֵהֶ֖ם קְדֹשִׁ֣ים תִּהְי֑וּ כִּ֣י קָד֔וֹשׁ אֲנִ֖י יְהֹוָ֥ה אֱלֹהֵיכֶֽם: ³אִ֣ישׁ אִמּ֤וֹ וְאָבִיו֙ תִּירָ֔אוּ וְאֶת־שַׁבְּתֹתַ֖י תִּשְׁמֹ֑רוּ אֲנִ֖י יְהֹוָ֥ה אֱלֹהֵיכֶֽם: ⁴אַל־תִּפְנוּ֙ אֶל־הָ֣אֱלִילִ֔ם וֵֽאלֹהֵי֙ מַסֵּכָ֔ה לֹ֥א תַעֲשׂ֖וּ לָכֶ֑ם אֲנִ֖י יְהֹוָ֥ה אֱלֹהֵיכֶֽם:

Leviticus 19:15–17

¹⁵לֹא־תַעֲשׂ֥וּ עָ֙וֶל֙ בַּמִּשְׁפָּ֔ט לֹא־תִשָּׂ֣א פְנֵי־דָ֔ל וְלֹ֥א תֶהְדַּ֖ר פְּנֵ֣י גָד֑וֹל בְּצֶ֖דֶק תִּשְׁפֹּ֥ט עֲמִיתֶֽךָ: ¹⁶לֹא־תֵלֵ֤ךְ רָכִיל֙ בְּעַמֶּ֔יךָ לֹ֥א תַעֲמֹ֖ד עַל־דַּ֣ם רֵעֶ֑ךָ אֲנִ֖י יְהֹוָֽה: ¹⁷לֹֽא־תִשְׂנָ֥א אֶת־אָחִ֖יךָ בִּלְבָבֶ֑ךָ הוֹכֵ֤חַ תּוֹכִ֙יחַ֙ אֶת־עֲמִיתֶ֔ךָ וְלֹא־תִשָּׂ֥א עָלָ֖יו חֵֽטְא:

Leviticus 19:33–34

³³וְכִֽי־יָג֧וּר אִתְּךָ֛ גֵּ֖ר בְּאַרְצְכֶ֑ם לֹ֥א תוֹנ֖וּ אֹתֽוֹ: ³⁴כְּאֶזְרָ֣ח מִכֶּ֗ם יִהְיֶ֤ה לָכֶם֙ הַגֵּ֣ר ׀ הַגָּ֣ר אִתְּכֶ֔ם וְאָהַבְתָּ֥ לוֹ֙ כָּמ֔וֹךָ כִּֽי־גֵרִ֥ים הֱיִיתֶ֖ם בְּאֶ֣רֶץ מִצְרָ֑יִם אֲנִ֖י יְהֹוָ֥ה אֱלֹהֵיכֶֽם:

reversing vav, *may also be translated as* and: —	וַ־, וְ־
	וַיְדַבֵּר, וְאָמַרְתָּ, וְאָהַבְתָּ
speak, talk *(A.I.E. Ch 6), appears in the following words:* וַיְדַבֵּר, דִּבֶּר —	דּ־ב־ר
to, toward *(B.I.F.B. Ch 3), also appears with pronoun ending:* אֲלֵהֶם —	אֶל
Moses *(A.I.E. Ch 4)* —	מֹשֶׁה
say, utter, tell *(B.I.F.B. Ch 1) appears in the following words:* לֵאמֹר, וְאָמַרְתָּ —	א־מ־ר
to, for *(attached preposition) (A.I.E. Ch 8), appears on the following words:* לֵאמֹר, לָכֶם, לוֹ —	ל־
all, every *(A.I.E. Ch 8)* —	כָּל
son, child *m (A.I.E. Ch 3), appears in plural word-pair form:* בְּנֵי —	בֵּן
Israel *m (A.I.E. Ch 1)* —	יִשְׂרָאֵל
their, them *(attached ending) (B.I.F.B. Ch 5), appears on the word* אֲלֵהֶם —	־הֶם
holy, sacred *adj (A.I.E. Ch 6)* —	קָדוֹשׁ
plural ending *(A.I.E. Ch 2), appears on the following words:* —	־ִים
	קָדָשִׁים, הָאֱלִילִם, גֵּרִים
be, exist *(B.I.F.B. Ch 1), appears in the following words:* —	ה־י־ה
	תִּהְיוּ, יִהְיֶה, הֱיִיתֶם
because, for; that *(T.I.F.T. Ch 3)* —	כִּי
I *(T.I.F.T. Ch 1)* —	אֲנִי
God *m (A.I.E. Ch 4), appears in the following words:* אֱלֹהֵיכֶם, וֵאלֹהֵי —	אֱלֹהִים
your, you *(attached ending) m pl (A.I.E. Ch 6), appears on the following words:* —	־כֶם
	אֱלֹהֵיכֶם, לָכֶם, בְּאַרְצְכֶם, מִכֶּם, אִתְכֶם
man *m (B.I.F.B. Ch 3)* —	אִישׁ

mother *f (A.I.E. Ch 5), appears with pronoun*
  ending: אִמּוֹ — אֵם

his, him *(attached ending) m sg (A.I.E. Ch 9), appears on the*
  following words: — וֹ־, ־יו

אִמּוֹ, וְאָבִיו, עָלָיו, אִתּוֹ, לוֹ

and *(attached prefix) (A.I.E. Ch 2), appears on the following words:* — וְ־, וּ־

וְאָבִיו, וְאֶת, וֵאלֹהֵי, וְלֹא, וְכִי

father, ancestor *m (A.I.E. Ch 5)* — אָב

fear, revere, be in awe *(T.I.F.T. Ch 1), appears in*
  the word תִּירְאוּ — י־ר־א

definite direct object marker (untranslatable) *(A.I.E. Ch 4),*
  appears four times, once with pronoun
  ending: אֹתוֹ — אֶת

plural ending *(A.I.E. Ch 2), appears on the*
  word שַׁבְּתֹתַי — וֹת־, ־ת

Shabbat, Sabbath *f (A.I.E. Ch 3), appears in plural with*
  pronoun ending: שַׁבְּתֹתַי — שַׁבָּת

my, me *(attached ending)*
  (T.I.F.T. Ch 3) — ־י

guard, keep, preserve *(A.I.E. Ch 3), appears in the*
  word תִּשְׁמְרוּ — שׁ־מ־ר

the *(attached prefix) (A.I.E. Ch 1), appears on the*
  following words: — הַ־, הָ־

הָאֱלִילִם, הַגֵּר, הַגֵּר

no, not *(B.I.F.B. Ch 3)* — לֹא

make, do, act *(A.I.E. Ch 7), appears in the*
  word תַּעֲשׂוּ — ע־שׂ־ה

with, in *(attached preposition) (A.I.E. Ch 6), appears on the*
  following words: — בְּ־

בַּמִּשְׁפָּט, בְּצֶדֶק, בְּעַמֶּיךָ, בִּלְבָבֶךָ, בְּאַרְצְכֶם, בָּאָרֶץ

face *m pl and f pl (B.I.F.B. Ch 1), appears in word-pair*
  form: פְּנֵי, פְּנֵי — פָּנִים

big, great *adj (A.I.E. Ch 5)* — גָּדוֹל

righteousness, justice *m (A.I.E. Ch 4)* — צֶדֶק

your, you *(attached ending) m sg (A.I.E. Ch 6),* appears on the
following words: — ךְ-

עֲמִיתֶךָ, בְּעַמֶּיךָ, רֵעֶךָ, אָחִיךָ, בִּלְבָבֶךָ, אִתְּךָ, כָּמוֹךָ

walk, go *(B.I.F.B. Ch 9),* appears in the
word תֵלֵךְ — ה-ל-ךְ

people, nation *m (A.I.E. Ch 4),* appears with
pronoun ending: עַמֶּיךָ — עַם

on, about *(A.I.E. Ch 8),* also appears with
pronoun ending: עָלָיו — עַל

blood *m (B.I.F.B. Ch 3)* — דַּם

friend, companion, fellow, neighbor *m (B.I.F.B. Ch 5),* appears
with pronoun ending: רֵעֶךָ — רֵעַ

brother *m (B.I.F.B. Ch 3),* appears with
pronoun ending: אָחִיךָ — אַח

heart *m (A.I.E. Ch 6),* appears with prefix and
pronoun ending: בִּלְבָבֶךָ — לֵבָב

with *(preposition) (B.I.F.B. Ch 3),* appears with pronoun
endings: אִתְּךָ, אִתְכֶם — אֵת

earth, land *f (A.I.E. Ch 3),* appears with prefixes and
endings: בְּאַרְצְכֶם, בָּאֶרֶץ — אֶרֶץ

like, as *(attached preposition) (A.I.E. Ch 7),* appears on the following
words: כְּאֶזְרָח, כָּמוֹךָ — כְּ-

from, than *(attached preposition) (A.I.E. Ch 10),* appears
on the word מִכֶּם — מִ-

love *(A.I.E. Ch 6),* appears in the
word וְאָהַבְתָּ — א-ה-ב

Egypt *(A.I.E. Ch 10)* — מִצְרָיִם

Translating the Torah Study Text [pages 58–60]

As your students work on their translations, the following comments may assist them:

1. The new Building Blocks for this unit (to be introduced in the next chapter) are the
   imperfect "you" forms. Our Torah Study Text is full of these forms, characterized by the
   prefix תּ and, if plural, the ending וּ. In this translation exercise section of our textbook, these forms are simply translated with the root meaning of the verb. This is
   because these forms can be translated as commands. For example, in the first paragraph

(verses 1–4), we find the following imperfect "you" forms:

קְדֹשִׁים תִּהְיוּ, which could be translated: "**Be holy**" *or* "**You shall be** holy."

אִישׁ אִמּוֹ וְאָבִיו תִּירָאוּ, which could be translated: "[Each] man **revere/fear** his mother and his father" *or* "**You shall revere/fear** [each] man his mother and his father."

וְאֶת־שַׁבְּתֹתַי תִּשְׁמֹרוּ which could be translated: **Keep** my Sabbaths *or* **You shall keep** my Sabbaths.

אַל־תִּפְנוּ אֶל־הָאֱלִילִם, which could be translated: "**Turn not** to the idols" *or* "**You shall not turn** to the idols."

וֵאלֹהֵי מַסֵּכָה לֹא תַעֲשׂוּ, which could be translated: "**Make not** gods of molten metal" *or* "**You shall not make** gods of molten metal."

2. As in the Torah Study Text of the last unit, there is a root doubled for emphasis in verse 17: הוֹכֵחַ תּוֹכִיחַ. This emphasis is lost in the JPS and ArtScroll translations. Everett Fox again preserves the repetition in his English rendition: "rebuke, yes, rebuke…," while the *Jerusalem Bible* inserts the word "certainly" for emphasis: "thou shalt certainly rebuke…."

3. The word כִּי, introduced in the last unit with the meaning *"because*," "for," or "that," is a grammatical particle that can be used in different combinations with a wide array of meanings. For example, in the Torah Study Text of Chapter 1, Jacob's ladder, it appears in verse 17 with the word אִם. The two-word phrase כִּי אִם there means "but" or "other than." And in verse 33 of our selection, it appears with the prefix וְ, with the meaning "and if" or "when."

[pages 60–62]

The opening verses of our Torah Study Text have a rhythmic quality that is lost in many English translations. Verses 2–4 all end with the words אֲנִי יְהֹוָה אֱלֹהֵיכֶם (the subject of the first Torah commentary cited in this chapter), but these constitute a concluding statement in verses 3 and 4, while in verse 2, the word אֲנִי is part of the preceding statement כִּי קָדוֹשׁ אֲנִי. Everett Fox's translation highlights this rhythmic quality by setting up each of verses 2–4 in a three-line poetic structure, with the third line containing the words "I, YHWH your God!" or "I am YHWH your God!"

In verse 16, the phrase לֹא תַעֲמֹד עַל־דַּם רֵעֶךָ is somewhat difficult to understand. The preposition עַל can have a variety of different meanings: "on," "over," "about," "above," "upon," "regarding," "concerning." None of these meanings clearly goes with the command לֹא תַעֲמֹד, "Stand not" or "You shall not stand," or with the object דַּם רֵעֶךָ, "the blood of your neighbor/fellow."

Three of our translations understand this phrase to mean that one should not stand aside while another is harmed, though even these three translations contain significant differences in terms of how broadly this prohibition is to be applied:

> ArtScroll *Chumash*: "You shall not stand aside while your fellow's blood is shed."
> Everett Fox: "You are not to stand by the blood of your neighbor."
> *Jerusalem Bible*: "neither shalt thou stand aside when mischief befalls thy neighbor."

The JPS translation follows a completely different understanding of "standing upon" the blood of your fellow: "Do not profit by the blood of your fellow."

Notice how the ArtScroll *Chumash* translates the word גֵּר in verses 33 and 34. In biblical Hebrew, the word means "sojourner" or "stranger," a nonnative residing among the people. In postbiblical Hebrew, the word came to be used to refer to proselytes, converts to Judaism. By translating the word with its postbiblical meaning, the ArtScroll *Chumash* links this passage to later teachings concerning the treatment of proselytes. This interpretation also has the effect of restricting the application of the command "you shall love him like yourself" to fellow Jews.

Vocabulary [page 63]

All the new vocabulary words are identified and highlighted within the Torah Study Text at the beginning of Chapter 6, on page 71.

1. The word לֵאמֹר is actually an infinitive construct form of the root א־מ־ר. Most often, though, it is translated as "saying," rather than as the infinitive to "say."
2. The word עֵדָה, "congregation/assembly/community," appears only in word-pair form: עֲדַת in verse 2.

The Hebrew Root [pages 63–65]

The first root letter נ drops out of all the imperfect forms of נ־שׂ־א. The word תִּשָּׂא appearing in verses 15 and 17 is a "you" imperfect form. (These forms will be introduced as the Building Blocks in the next chapter.)

The forms of the root ע־מ־ד contain the slight variations in vowels characteristic of verbs with first root letter ע. Its forms are the same as those from the root ע־ב־ד. The word תַעֲמֹד in verse 16 is a "you" imperfect form. The word תַעֲמֹד is also included in the list of words and expressions derived from this root, because it is part of the phrase used in synagogue for calling someone to the Torah. This is a good example of how an imperfect verb form can have very different meanings as a command: "You shall [not] stand," versus describing an action wished or urged: "Let so-and-so stand."

Exercises

Exercise 2 [page 67]

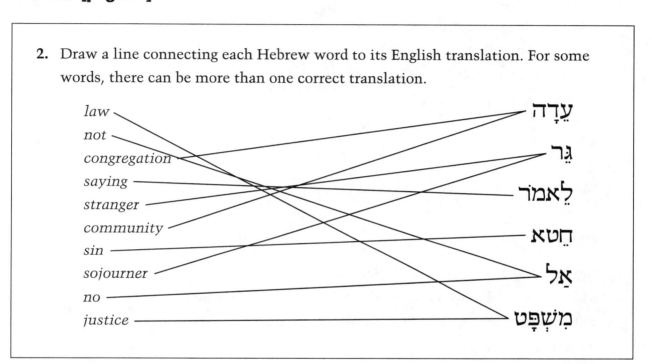

2. Draw a line connecting each Hebrew word to its English translation. For some words, there can be more than one correct translation.

law	עֵדָה
not	גֵּר
congregation	לֵאמֹר
saying	חֵטְא
stranger	אֶל
community	מִשְׁפָּט
sin	
sojourner	
no	
justice	

Exercise 3 [page 67]

3. The following are plural forms of words introduced as vocabulary in this chapter. Draw a line connecting each plural word to its singular form. Translate both into English.

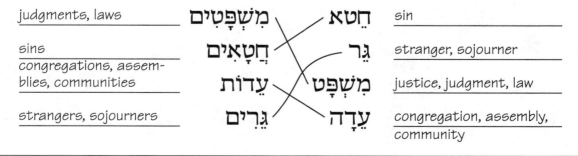

judgments, laws	מִשְׁפָּטִים	חֵטְא	sin
sins	חֲטָאִים	גֵּר	stranger, sojourner
congregations, assemblies, communities	עֵדוֹת	מִשְׁפָּט	justice, judgment, law
strangers, sojourners	גֵּרִים	עֵדָה	congregation, assembly, community

Exercise 4 [page 68]

a. in the midst of/within the community/congregation/assembly

    in the eyes of the community/congregation/assembly

    the community/congregation/assembly of Israel

    the community/congregation/assembly of God

    my community/congregation/assembly

b. truth and justice

    justice and righteousness

    spirit of justice

    guards/guardians/keepers of law/justice

    the place of law/judgment/justice

c. great sins

    my sins

    his sins

    our sins

    your *(m pl)* sins

d. the soul/mind of the stranger/sojourner

    justice/law of [the] stranger/sojourner *or* a stranger's law/justice

    a strange/sojourning man (*literally:* a man a stranger)

    your *(m sg)* stranger/sojourner

    like a stranger/sojourner in the land

e. God blessed them saying...

    The king commanded the slave/servant saying...

    God said to Jacob, saying...

    He spoke with the man, saying...

    The word of the Eternal was toward me (*i.e.,* upon me) saying...

Exercise 5 [page 69]

Translation	Form	Root	Verb
lift/bear/carry *m sg*	participle	נ־שׂ־א	נוֹשֵׂא
stand *f sg*	participle	ע־מ־ד	עוֹמֶדֶת
see *f pl*	participle	ר־א־ה	רוֹאוֹת
she will/shall/may come *or* let her come	imperfect	ב־ו־א	תָּבוֹא
they will/shall/may stand *or* let them stand	imperfect	ע־מ־ד	יַעַמְדוּ
I will/shall/may work/serve *or* let me...	imperfect	ע־ב־ד	אֶעֱבֹד
I will/shall/may be *or* let me be	imperfect	ה־י־ה	אֶהְיֶה
I knew/did know/was ...ing/had .../have ...	perfect	י־ד־ע	יָדַעְתִּי
I walked/went did .../was ...ing/had .../have ...	perfect	ה־ל־ך	הָלַכְתִּי
I lifted/bore/carried did .../was .../had .../have ...	perfect	נ־שׂ־א	נָשָׂאתִי
I feared/was in awe of did .../was .../had .../have ...	perfect	י־ר־א	יָרֵאתִי
cause to stand/erect/set up/establish *m pl*	participle	ע־מ־ד	מַעֲמִידִים

Notes on

Torah Study Text: Vocabulary and Root Review [page 71]

Vocabulary words that appear in our Torah Study Text in variant forms or with prefixes or suffixes attached were noted in the Vocabulary section of the previous chapter of this Teacher's Guide. The various forms of the new roots נ־שׂ־א and ע־מ־ד were explained in the Hebrew Root section of the previous chapter of this Teacher's Guide.

Building Blocks

"You" Verb Forms [page 72]

You may want to refer your students to the Grammar Enrichment charts in *Aleph Isn't Enough*, pages 14 and 156, which include the four Hebrew "you" pronouns:

אַתֶּן *f pl*　אַתֶּם *m pl*　אַתְּ *f sg*　אַתָּה *m sg*

It may also be helpful to remind your students that they have already been encountering singular and plural "you" forms with the pronoun endings ךָ and כֶם.

As mentioned in *Aleph Isn't Enough*, Chapter 6, masculine plural forms are used for both all-male and mixed gender groups. Masculine singular forms are used when addressing a single male, but can also be interpreted as addressing a single individual of unspecified gender, as in certain biblical commandments.

Perfect Forms [page 72]

The regular *masculine singular* perfect ending is תָּ, and the regular *masculine plural* perfect ending is תֶּם. The תָ and תֶם endings are variations that occur when the final root letter is א or ה.

The regular פָּעַל *masculine singular* perfect form is ▢▢▢תָ. (In the well-known prayer *V'ahavta*, there is a reversing *vav* attached to אָהַבְתָּ, producing the translation "you shall love.") The regular פָּעַל *masculine plural* perfect form is ▢▢▢תֶּם.

The regular פָּעַל *masculine singular* perfect form is ▢▢▢תָּ, and the regular *masculine plural* perfect form is: ▢▢▢תֶּם.

The regular הִפְעִיל *masculine singular* perfect form is: ה▢▢▢תָּ and the regular הִפְעִיל *masculine plural* perfect form is ה▢▢▢תֶּם. The examples הֶעֱמַדְתָּ and הֶעֱמַדְתֶּם contain a slight variation in the vowels caused by the first root letter ע.

Imperfect Forms [page 73]

The imperfect "you" forms can be used in Hebrew to express commands. Our Torah Study text is filled with examples of imperfect "you" forms used for commands. Similarly, a negative command can be expressed by using an imperfect "you" form with the negative term אַל, introduced as a new vocabulary word in this unit.

There are many variations in the vowels of imperfect forms, caused by various root letters.

The regular פָּעַל *masculine singular* imperfect form is תִּ◌◌ֹ◌, and the regular פָּעַל *masculine plural* imperfect form is תִּ◌◌ְ◌וּ. However, most of the verb roots introduced thus far do not follow these regular patterns, but contain some variation in vowels due to the root letters ע, ח, ה, א, or י or ו.

The regular פָּעַל *masculine singular* imperfect form is תִּ◌◌ַ◌, and the regular פָּעַל *masculine plural* imperfect form is תִּ◌◌ַ◌וּ.

The regular הִפְעִיל *masculine singular* imperfect form is תַּ◌◌ִי◌, and the regular הִפְעִיל *masculine plural* imperfect form is תַּ◌◌ִי◌וּ. The examples תַּעֲמִיד and תַּעֲמִידוּ contain a slight variation in the vowels caused by the first root letter ע.

Torah Study Text with Building Blocks [pages 73–75]

The Torah Study text contains many singular and plural "you" forms from unfamiliar roots. Reassure your students that they are not expected to know all these roots. It is enough for them to be able to recognize from the prefixes and/or endings that these are singular or plural imperfect or perfect "you" forms.

[page 75–76]

You may wish to point out to your students that the imperfect forms of the root הָ־לַ־ךְ in both the פָּעַל and הִפְעִיל patterns are like those verbs with the first root letter י. It also may be helpful to note that, in the הִפְעִיל pattern, verbs with first root letter י have a vowel וֹ in place of the consonant י.

Additional Reading and Translation Practice [pages 77–81]

1. Psalm 121 is included in the memorial service in *Gates of Prayer: The New Union Prayerbook* on page 546–547.

2. עַל שְׁלֹשָׁה דְבָרִים is included in the gender-sensitive *Gates of Prayer* on page 141.

3. לְמַעַן תִּזְכְּרוּ (Numbers 15:40–41) is included in the gender-sensitive *Gates of Prayer* on page 52.

4. The Shabbat evening קִדּוּשׁ is included in the gender-sensitive *Gates of Prayer* on page 165.

5. Deuteronomy 4:39 (included in the עָלֵינוּ) can be found in the gender-sensitive *Gates of Prayer* on page 148.

6. בִּרְכַּת הַמָּזוֹן can be found in *On the Doorposts of Your House* on pages 9–18. The excerpt included in our exercise is on page 12.

Exercises

Exercise 1 [page 81]

a. Hear/listen not! (Do not hear/listen!) *or* You *(m sg)* shall not hear/listen.

Hear/listen not! (Do not hear/listen!) *or* You *(m pl)* shall not hear/listen.

Fear not! (Do not fear!) *or* You *(m sg)* shall not fear.

Fear not! (Do not fear!) *or* You *(m pl)* shall not fear.

See not! (Do not see!) *or* You *(m sg)* shall not see.

b. Eat not! (Do not eat!) *or* You *(m pl)* shall not eat.

Eat not! (Do not eat!) *or* You *(m sg)* shall not eat.

Come not! (Do not come!) *or* You *(m sg)* shall not come.

Come not! (Do not come!) *or* You *(m pl)* shall not come.

Build not! (Do not build!) *or* You *(m pl)* shall not build.

c. Walk/Go not! (Do not walk/go!) *or* You *(m sg)* shall not walk/go.

Walk/Go not! (Do not walk/go!) *or* You *(m pl)* shall not walk/go.

Help not! (Do not help!) *or* You *(m sg)* shall not help.

Help not! (Do not help!) *or* You *(m pl)* shall not help.

Speak not! (Do not speak!) *or* You *(m pl)* shall not speak.

Exercise 2 [page 82]

Translation	Form	Root	Singular	Plural
you worked/served	perfect	ע־ב־ד	עָבַדְתָּ	בָּאתֶם
you took	perfect	ל־ק־ח	לָקַחְתָּ	רְאִיתֶם
you went/walked	perfect	ה־ל־ך	הָלַכְתָּ	הֱיִיתֶם
you will/shall/may build	imperfect	ב־נ־ה	תִּבְנֶה	נְשָׂאתֶם
you will/shall/may stand	imperfect	ע־ל־ה	תַּעֲלֶה	תַּעַמְדוּ
you feared/were in awe of	perfect	י־ר־א	יָרֵאתָ	תִּירְאוּ
you saw	perfect	ר־א־ה	רָאִיתָ	תִּבְנוּ
you will/shall/may fear	imperfect	י־ר־א	תִּירָא	עֲבַדְתֶּם
you were	perfect	ה־י־ה	הָיִיתָ	הוֹשַׁבְתֶּם
you came	perfect	ב־ו־א	בָּאתָ	צִוִּיתֶם
you lifted/bore/carried	perfect	נ־שׂ־א	נָשָׂאתָ	תְּהַלְלוּ
you will/shall/may stand	imperfect	ע־מ־ד	תַּעֲמֹד	לְקַחְתֶּם
you will/shall/may praise	imperfect	ה־ל־ל	תְּהַלֵּל	יְרֵאתֶם
you commanded	perfect	צ־ו־ה	צִוִּיתָ	הֲלַכְתֶּם
you seated/caused to dwell	perfect	י־שׁ־ב	הוֹשַׁבְתָּ	תַּעֲלוּ

Torah Study Text: Deuteronomy 5:6–7, 12–18 [pages 87–88]

Following are all the words, roots, endings, and prefixes appearing in Deuteronomy 5:6–7, 12–18 that have already been introduced. The book and chapter in which they were introduced is indicated in parentheses.

Deuteronomy 5:6–7

‎⁶אָנֹכִי יְהֹוָה אֱלֹהֶיךָ אֲשֶׁר הוֹצֵאתִיךָ מֵאֶרֶץ מִצְרַיִם מִבֵּית עֲבָדִים:

‎⁷לֹא יִהְיֶה־לְךָ אֱלֹהִים אֲחֵרִים עַל־פָּנָי:

Deuteronomy 5:12–18

‎¹²שָׁמוֹר אֶת־יוֹם הַשַּׁבָּת לְקַדְּשׁוֹ כַּאֲשֶׁר צִוְּךָ יְהֹוָה אֱלֹהֶיךָ: ¹³שֵׁשֶׁת יָמִים תַּעֲבֹד וְעָשִׂיתָ כָּל־מְלַאכְתֶּךָ: ¹⁴וְיוֹם הַשְּׁבִיעִי שַׁבָּת לַיהֹוָה אֱלֹהֶיךָ לֹא־תַעֲשֶׂה כָל־מְלָאכָה אַתָּה וּבִנְךָ־וּבִתֶּךָ וְעַבְדְּךָ־וַאֲמָתֶךָ וְשׁוֹרְךָ וַחֲמֹרְךָ וְכָל־בְּהֶמְתֶּךָ וְגֵרְךָ אֲשֶׁר בִּשְׁעָרֶיךָ לְמַעַן יָנוּחַ עַבְדְּךָ וַאֲמָתְךָ כָּמוֹךָ: ¹⁵וְזָכַרְתָּ כִּי עֶבֶד הָיִיתָ בְּאֶרֶץ מִצְרַיִם וַיֹּצִאֲךָ יְהֹוָה אֱלֹהֶיךָ מִשָּׁם בְּיָד חֲזָקָה וּבִזְרֹעַ נְטוּיָה עַל־כֵּן צִוְּךָ יְהֹוָה אֱלֹהֶיךָ לַעֲשׂוֹת אֶת־יוֹם הַשַּׁבָּת: ¹⁶כַּבֵּד אֶת־אָבִיךָ וְאֶת־אִמֶּךָ כַּאֲשֶׁר צִוְּךָ יְהֹוָה אֱלֹהֶיךָ לְמַעַן יַאֲרִיכֻן יָמֶיךָ וּלְמַעַן יִיטַב לָךְ עַל הָאֲדָמָה אֲשֶׁר־יְהֹוָה אֱלֹהֶיךָ נֹתֵן לָךְ: ¹⁷לֹא תִּרְצָח וְלֹא תִּנְאָף וְלֹא תִּגְנֹב וְלֹא־תַעֲנֶה בְרֵעֲךָ עֵד שָׁוְא: ¹⁸וְלֹא תַחְמֹד אֵשֶׁת רֵעֶךָ וְלֹא תִתְאַוֶּה בֵּית רֵעֶךָ שָׂדֵהוּ וְעַבְדּוֹ וַאֲמָתוֹ שׁוֹרוֹ וַחֲמֹרוֹ וְכֹל אֲשֶׁר לְרֵעֶךָ:

I *(T.I.F.T. Ch 1)*	אָנֹכִי
God *m (A.I.E. Ch 4)*, appears with pronoun ending אֱלֹהֶיךָ	אֱלֹהִים
your, you *(attached ending) m sg (A.I.E. Ch 6)*, appears on the following words:	ךָ

אֱלֹהֶיךָ, הוֹצֵאתִיךָ, לָךְ, צִוְּךָ, מְלַאכְתֶּךָ, וּבִנְךָ, וּבִתֶּךָ, וְעַבְדְּךָ,
וַאֲמָתֶךָ, וְשׁוֹרְךָ, וַחֲמֹרְךָ, בְּהֶמְתֶּךָ, וְגֵרְךָ, בִּשְׁעָרֶיךָ, וַאֲמָתֶךָ,
כָּמוֹךָ, וַיֹּצִאֲךָ, אָבִיךָ, אִמֶּךָ, יָמֶיךָ, לָךְ, בְּרֵעֲךָ, רֵעֶךָ, לְרֵעֶךָ

who, that, which *(A.I.E. Ch 8)*	אֲשֶׁר
הִפְעִיל: cause to go out, bring out *(B.I.F.B. Ch 10)*, appears in the following words:	יצ־א

הוֹצֵאתִיךָ, וַיֹּצִאֲךָ

perfect I ending *(T.I.F.T. Ch 4)*, appears in the word הוֹצֵאתִיךָ	תִי
earth, land *f (A.I.E. Ch 3)*	אֶרֶץ
from, than *(attached preposition) (A.I.E. Ch 10)*, appears on the following words:	מֵי, מִי

מֵאֶרֶץ, מִבֵּית, מִשָּׁם

Egypt *(A.I.E. Ch 10)*	מִצְרַיִם
house *m (A.I.E. Ch 6)*, appears in word-pair form: בֵּית	בַּיִת
slave, bondsman, servant *m (A.I.E. Ch 10)*, appears with endings:	עֶבֶד

עֲבָדִים, עַבְדְּךָ, וְעַבְדוֹ

plural ending, appears on the following words:	ים

עֲבָדִים, אֲחֵרִים, יָמִים

no, not *(B.I.F.B. Ch 3)*	לֹא
be, exist *(B.I.F.B. Ch 1)*, appears in the following words:	ה־י־ה

יִהְיֶה, הָיִיתָ

to, for *(attached preposition) (A.I.E. Ch 8)*, appears on the following words:	לְ

לָךְ, לְקַדְּשׁוֹ, לַיהוָֹה, לַעֲשׂוֹת, לְרֵעֶךָ

on, about (A.I.E. Ch 8)   —   עַל

face *m pl* and *f pl (B.I.F.B. Ch 1)*, appears with
pronoun ending: פָּנַי   —   פָּנִים

guard, keep, preserve *(A.I.E. Ch 3)*, appears in
the word שָׁמוֹר   —   שׁ־מ־ר

definite direct object marker (untranslatable) *(A.I.E. Ch 4)*,
appears four times   —   אֶת

day *m (A.I.E. Ch 3)*, also appears
as יָמִים, יָמֶיךָ   —   יוֹם

the *(attached prefix) (A.I.E. Ch 1)*, appears on the
following words: —   ־הַ

הַשַּׁבָּת, הַשְּׁבִיעִי, הָאֲדָמָה

Shabbat, Sabbath *f (A.I.E. Ch 3)*   —   שַׁבָּת

make holy, sanctify *(A.I.E. Ch 7)*, appears in
the word לְקַדְּשׁוֹ   —   ק־ד־שׁ

his, him, its, it *(attached ending) m sg (A.I.E. Ch 9)*, appears on the
following words: —   ־וֹ, ־הוּ

לְקַדְּשׁוֹ, שָׂדֵהוּ, וְעַבְדּוֹ, וַאֲמָתוֹ, שׁוֹרוֹ, וַחֲמֹרוֹ

command, order *(A.I.E. Ch 8)*, appears in
the word צִוְּךָ   —   צ־ו־ה

work, serve *(B.I.F.B. Ch 3)*, appears in
the word תַּעֲבֹד   —   ע־ב־ד

imperfect you *m sg* prefix, appears on the
following words: —   ־תְּ, ת־

תַּעֲבֹד, תַּעֲשֶׂה, תִּרְצַח, תִּנְאָף, תִּגְנֹב, תַּעֲנֶה, תַּחְמֹד, תִתְאַוֶּה

reversing vav, may also be translated
as *and:*   —   ־וַ, ־וְ

וְעָשִׂיתָ, וְזָכַרְתָּ, וַיֹּצִאֲךָ

make, do, act *(A.I.E. Ch 7)*, appears in the
following words: —   ע־שׂ־ה

וְעָשִׂיתָ, תַּעֲשֶׂה, לַעֲשׂוֹת

perfect you *m sg* ending, appears on the
following words: —   ־תָּ, ־תָ

וְעָשִׂיתָ, וְזָכַרְתָּ, הָיִיתָ

all, every *(A.I.E. Ch 8)*	—	כָּל, כָּל, כֹּל
and *(attached prefix) (A.I.E. Ch 2)*, appears on the following words:	—	וְ־, וַ־, וּ־

וְיוֹם, וּבִנְךָ, וּבִתֶּךָ, וְעַבְדְּךָ, וַאֲמָתֶךָ, וְשׁוֹרְךָ, וַחֲמֹרְךָ, וְכָל, וְגֵרְךָ, וַאֲמָתְךָ, וּבְזַרְעֲ, וְאֶת, וּלְמַעַן, וְלֹא, וְעַבְדּוֹ, וַאֲמָתוֹ, וַחֲמֹרוֹ, וְכֹל

you *m sg (A.I.E. Ch 1)*	—	אַתָּה
son, child *m (A.I.E. Ch 3)*	—	בֵּן
stranger, sojourner *m (T.I.F.T. Ch 5)*	—	גֵּר
with, in *(attached preposition) (A.I.E. Ch 6)*, appears on the following words:	—	בְּ־, בַּ־

בִּשְׁעָרֶיךָ, בְּאֶרֶץ, בְּיָד, בְּרֵעֲךָ

like, as *(A.I.E. Ch 7)*, appears with pronoun ending: כָּמוֹךָ	—	כְּמוֹ
remember *(A.I.E. Ch 5)*, appears in the word וְזָכַרְתָּ	—	ז־כ־ר
there *(B.I.F.B. Ch 5)*, appears with prefix: מִשָּׁם	—	שָׁם
hand *f (A.I.E. Ch 6)*	—	יָד
father, ancestor *m (A.I.E. Ch 5)*, appears with pronoun ending: אָבִיךָ	—	אַב
mother *f (A.I.E. Ch 5)*, appears with pronoun ending: אִמֶּךָ	—	אֵם
earth, ground, land *f (A.I.E. Ch 8)*	—	אֲדָמָה
give, grant, permit *(A.I.E. Ch 4)*, appears as a participle: נֹתֵן	—	נ־ת־ן
friend, companion, fellow, neighbor *m (B.I.F.B. Ch 5)*	—	רֵעַ
woman, wife *f (B.I.F.B. Ch 3)*, appears in word-pair form: אֵשֶׁת	—	אִשָּׁה

Translating the Torah Study Text [pages 88–90]

As your students work on their translations, the following comments may assist them:

1. We have already seen many examples of pronoun endings attached to verbs, as in צִוְּךָ, "[he] commanded you," in verses 12, 16, and 17. (This is the הוּא perfect form צִוָּה

with the pronoun ךָ attached and the final הָ dropped.) Such pronoun endings can also be added to verbs that have a reversing *vav* attached, as in verse 16: וַיּוֹצִאֲךָ, "[he] brought you out." (This is יוֹצִיא, the הִפְעִיל imperfect הוּא form of the root י־צ־א, with a reversing *vav* and the pronoun ךָ added.)

Pronoun endings can even be added to verbs that already have a verb (perfect or imperfect) ending added, such as הוֹצֵאתִיךָ, "I brought you out," in verse 5, which has both the אֲנִי, "I," perfect ending תִי and the pronoun ending ךָ.

2. The words לֹא יִהְיֶה לְךָ (literally: "will not be to you") is a type of grammatical construction indicating possession, which will be explained in the Building Blocks section of this unit, in the next chapter.

[pages 91–93]

There are a few details in the ArtScroll translation of our Torah Study Text that reflect its more traditional orientation.

In verse 7, the ArtScroll *Chumash* is the only translation to render אֱלֹהִים אֲחֵרִים as, "the gods of others." (Grammatically, "the gods of others," would be a more appropriate translation for a word pair such as אֱלֹהֵי הָאֲחֵרִים.) The other three translations all render אֱלֹהִים אֲחֵרִים as "other gods," which is a grammatically appropriate translation for such a noun and adjective combination. It can be somewhat problematic, however, from a traditional viewpoint, to have the one and only God implicitly acknowledging the existence of other gods by commanding us not to worship them. The ArtScroll translation "You shall not recognize the gods of others in My presence" avoids this problem.

In verse 14, the ArtScroll *Chumash* translates the word גֵּר, "stranger/sojourner," with its postbiblical meaning "convert." (We saw a similiar translation of גֵּר as "proselyte" in the ArtScroll *Chumash* translation of our last Torah Study text.) The other three translations all render this word as "stranger" or "sojourner." The ArtScroll translation "convert" reflects the traditional view of Shabbat as a sign of the special covenant between God and the Jewish people, whereby Shabbat observance has been given to Jews (whether Jews-by-choice or Jews-by-birth) but not to non-Jews.

Vocabulary [pages 93–94]

All the new vocabulary words are identified and highlighted within the Torah Study Text at the beginning of Chapter 8, on page 101.

1. The adjective אַחֵר appears in a masculine plural form in verse 7.

2. The final ה in the word מְלָאכָה becomes a ת when pronoun endings are added, as in מְלַאכְתֶּךָ in verse 12.

3. The word בַּת will be familiar to most students from the term for a young female who has come of age and the ceremony that marks this transition in life: בַּת מִצְוָה. The vowel changes when pronoun endings are attached, as in וּבִתֶּךָ in verse 14.

4. The word שַׁעַר appears in verse 14 with a prefix and ending: בִּשְׁעָרֶיךָ. You may wish to point out to your students that a plural word-pair form of שַׁעַר appears on the cover of the Reform prayer book: שַׁעֲרֵי תְּפִלָּה, *"Gates of Prayer."*

Hebrew Root [pages 94–95]

In the last chapter, we introduced the imperfect "you" forms, which can be used in Hebrew to indicate commands. There also exist command forms for each verb pattern, which we have not taught in this book. The form of the root כ־ב־ד that appears in our Torah Study text in verse 16 is such a command form.

The root כ־ב־ד does exist in the פָּעַל pattern (with the meaning "be heavy/weighty") and in the הִפְעִיל pattern (with the meanings "make heavy" and "cause to be honored"). Because it appears less often in those patterns, we have not introduced those forms in our text.

The root נ־ו־ח has the usual variations caused by the middle root letter ו, which drops out in the perfect and participle forms and is replaced by the וּ vowel in the פָּעַל imperfect forms. In the הִפְעִיל pattern, the root נ־ו־ח has two different conjugations, with differing meanings: מֵנִיחַ, "make rest," and מַנִּיחַ, "put/place/leave alone/allow/permit." To simplify the learning, we have only presented the first meaning. This first meaning also has two possible conjugations in the perfect: הֲנִיחוֹתִי, etc., as well as הֵנַחְתִּי. Again, to simplify our presentation, we only included the latter in the exercises and verb charts in this book.

Exercises

Exercise 2 [page 98]

2. Draw a line connecting each Hebrew word to its English translation. For some words, there can be more than one correct translation.

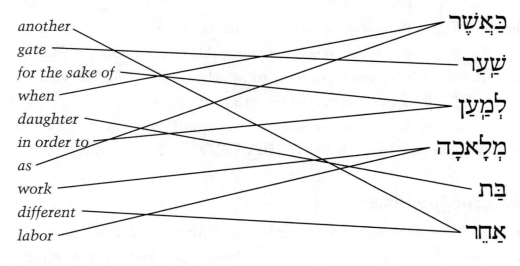

another
gate
for the sake of
when
daughter
in order to
as
work
different
labor

כַּאֲשֶׁר
שַׁעַר
לְמַעַן
מְלָאכָה
בַּת
אַחֵר

Exercise 3 [page 98]

3. The following are plural forms of words introduced as vocabulary in this chapter. Draw a line connecting each plural word to its singular form. Translate both into English.

daughters

others, different [ones]

gates

work, labors, occupations

בָּנוֹת
אֲחֵרִים
שְׁעָרִים
מְלָאכוֹת

מְלָאכָה
שַׁעַר
בַּת
אַחֵר

work, labor, occupation

gate

daughter

other, another, different

Exercise 4 [pages 98–99]

a. daughter of Zion
   daughters of Canaan
   their daughters
   my daughter
   our daughter

b. the gate of heaven
   the gates of Jerusalem
   gates of righteousness
   your *(m sg)* gates
   your *(m pl)* gates

c. for the sake of his name (*This phrase appears in the* Avot *prayer, in the gender-sensitive* Gates of Prayer *on page 56.)*
   for the sake of my brothers and friends (*This phrase appears in Psalm 122:8 and has been set to music.)*
   so that you *(m pl)* may remember (*This phrase opens the paragraph following the* V'ahavta *in the Reform liturgy, found in the gender-sensitive* Gates of Prayer *on page 52.)*
   for the sake of your *(m sg)* life
   for the sake of his covenant

d. his work/occupation/labor
   from all his work/occupation/labor *(This phrase appears in the* Vay'chulu *paragraph, Genesis 2:1–3, found in the Shabbat liturgy in the gender-sensitive* Gates of Prayer *on page 59.)*
   your *(m sg)* work/occupation/labor
   eternal work/labor (work/occupation/labor of eternities/worlds/universes)
   the work/occupation/labor of his neighbor/friend/companion/fellow

e. a different/another seed
   a different/another heart
   a different/another spirit
   a different/another year
   different/other days

f. as/according as/when I have spoken

as/according as/when the lord commanded

as/according as you (m pl) have heard

as/according as/when he did

as/according as/when you (m sg) will/may/shall see

Exercise 5 [pages 99–100]

Translation	Form	Root	Verb
come (m pl)	participle	ב־ו־א	בָּאִים
rest (m pl)	participle	נ־ו־ח	נָחִים
cause to rest/pacify/calm (m pl)	participle	נ־ו־ח	מְנִיחִים
honor/respect (m pl)	participle	כ־ב־ד	מְכַבְּדִים
he/it will/shall/may rest or let him/it rest	imperfect	נ־ו־ח	יָנוּחַ
you (m pl) will/shall/may rest	imperfect	נ־ו־ח	תָּנוּחוּ
you (m pl) will/shall/may honor/respect	imperfect	כ־ב־ד	תְכַבְּדוּ
I will/shall/may honor/respect or let me...	imperfect	כ־ב־ד	אֲכַבֵּד
you (m sg) lifted/bore/carried/did ...were .../had ...	perfect	נ־שׂ־א	נָשָׂאתָ
you (m sg) rested/did .../were ...ing/had .../have ...	perfect	נ־ו־ח	נַחְתָּ
you (m pl) rested/did .../were ...ing/had .../have ...	perfect	נ־ו־ח	נַחְתֶּם
you (m sg) caused to rest/pacified/calmed	perfect	נ־ו־ח	הֲנַחְתָּ

Notes on

Torah Study Text: Vocabulary and Root Review [page 101]

Vocabulary words that appear in our Torah Study Text in variant forms or with prefixes or suffixes attached were noted in the Vocabulary section of the previous chapter of this Teacher's Guide. The various forms of the new roots נ־ו־ח and כ־ב־ד were explained in the Hebrew Root section of the previous chapter of this Teacher's Guide.

Building Blocks [pages 102–103]

לְשָׂרָה בַּת, "Sarah has a daughter," is a classical Hebrew construction. In modern Hebrew, the preposition לְ is not used by itself to express "have." In the modern Hebrew present tense, the preposition לְ appears with either יֵשׁ, "there is," or אֵין, "there is not":

Sarah has a daughter.	—	יֵשׁ לְשָׂרָה בַּת.
Sarah does not have a daughter.	—	אֵין לְשָׂרָה בַּת.

In the modern Hebrew past and future tense, the preposition לְ appears with forms of the root ה־י־ה, like the classical Hebrew constructions.

[page 103]

The modern Hebrew way of expressing possession with the word שֶׁל, "of," is derived from the classical Hebrew construction אֲשֶׁר לְ. The word שֶׁל is a post-biblical word, a combination of the prefix שֶׁ (a short form of the word אֲשֶׁר, introduced in Chapter 8 of *Aleph Isn't Enough*) and the preposition לְ.

Additional Reading and Translation Practice [pages 104–108]

1. יוֹם זֶה לְיִשְׂרָאֵל is found in *On the Doorposts of Your House* on page 46.

2. אֲדוֹן עוֹלָם is found in the gender-sensitive *Gates of Prayer* on page 156.

3. לְךָ יְיָ (I Chronicles 29:11) is found in the gender-sensitive *Gates of Prayer* on page 143.

4. יִגְדַּל is found in the gender-sensitive *Gates of Prayer* on pages 157–158.

5. אֱמֶת וְיַצִּיב is found in the gender-sensitive *Gates of Prayer* on page 112.

6. As part of the Rosh HaShanah Haftarah reading, I Samuel 1:1–2 can be found on page 128 of the *Gates of Repentance*. Verse 2 provides a good example of the flexibility of tenses in biblical Hebrew. The phrase וְלוֹ שְׁתֵּי נָשִׁים, "and to him two wives," clearly should be rendered in English as "he **had** two wives," and not "he **has** two wives," even though there is no verb indicating tense in the Hebrew. Similarly the phrase וּלְחַנָּה אֵין יְלָדִים, "and to Chanah there are not children," should be understood as "Chanah **had** no children," even though the word אֵין, "there is/are not," appears in the Hebrew instead of לֹא, "not," and הָיוּ, the perfect form of the root ה־י־ה.

Exercises

Exercise 1 [pages 108–109]

1. In each of the following sentences, circle the one form in the parentheses that is grammatically correct. Translate.

   a. (יֵשׁ, הָיוּ, הָיְתָה) לִי בֵּן.
   I have {There is to me} a son. _____

   b. לְרָחֵל (הָיָה, הָיְתָה, הָיוּ) אֵם טוֹבָה.
   Rachel had {To Rachel was} _____
   a good mother.

   c. (הָיָה, הָיוּ, יִהְיֶה) לָנוּ עֵצִים אַחַר שַׁעֲרֵנוּ.
   We had {Were to us} _____
   trees behind our gate.

   d. לָעָם (הָיְתָה, לֹא תִהְיֶה, יֵשׁ) נָבִיא.
   The people/nation has {To the _____
   people/nation there is} a prophet.

   e. (יִהְיוּ, לֹא הָיְתָה, לֹא הָיוּ) לְאַבְרָהָם מְזוּזָה בְּבֵיתוֹ. _____
   Abraham did not have {There was not to Abraham} a doorpost in his house.

   f. (לֹא הָיָה, אֵין, לֹא הָיְתָה) לָכֶם עֲבָדִים רַבִּים.
   You do not have _____
   {There are not to you} many slaves.

   g. (יֵשׁ, הָיוּ, לֹא יִהְיֶה) רְפוּאָה לַחוֹלִים.
   There is a cure for the sick. _____
   or The sick [ones] have a cure.

   h. (יִהְיֶה, יִהְיוּ, תִּהְיֶה) לְךָ מִשְׁפָּחָה גְּדוֹלָה.
   You will/may have _____
   {Will/may be to you} a big/great family.

   i. (תִּהְיֶה, לֹא יִהְיֶה, הָיוּ) לָנוּ דָם בְּיָדֵינוּ.
   We will/shall/may not have _____
   {Not will/shall/may be to us} blood on our hands.

   j. (יִהְיוּ, הָיָה, תִּהְיֶה) לָהֶם רַחֲמִים בְּנַפְשׁוֹתֵיהֶם.
   They will/shall/ _____
   may have or Let them have or May they have {Will/shall/may be to them}
   compassion/mercy in their souls/minds.

Torah Study Text: Deuteronomy 30:11–16, 19 [page 114]

Following are all the words, roots, endings, and prefixes appearing in Deuteronomy 30:11–16, 19 that have already been introduced. The book and chapter in which they were introduced is indicated in parentheses.

Deuteronomy 30:11–16

¹¹כִּי הַמִּצְוָה הַזֹּאת אֲשֶׁר אָנֹכִי מְצַוְּךָ הַיּוֹם לֹא־נִפְלֵאת הִוא מִמְּךָ וְלֹא־רְחֹקָה הִוא: ¹²לֹא בַשָּׁמַיִם הִוא לֵאמֹר מִי יַעֲלֶה־לָּנוּ הַשָּׁמַיְמָה וְיִקָּחֶהָ לָּנוּ וְיַשְׁמִעֵנוּ אֹתָהּ וְנַעֲשֶׂנָּה: ¹³וְלֹא־מֵעֵבֶר לַיָּם הִוא לֵאמֹר מִי יַעֲבָר־לָנוּ אֶל־עֵבֶר הַיָּם וְיִקָּחֶהָ לָּנוּ וְיַשְׁמִעֵנוּ אֹתָהּ וְנַעֲשֶׂנָּה: ¹⁴כִּי־קָרוֹב אֵלֶיךָ הַדָּבָר מְאֹד בְּפִיךָ וּבִלְבָבְךָ לַעֲשֹׂתוֹ: ¹⁵רְאֵה נָתַתִּי לְפָנֶיךָ הַיּוֹם אֶת־הַחַיִּים וְאֶת־הַטּוֹב וְאֶת־הַמָּוֶת וְאֶת־הָרָע: ¹⁶אֲשֶׁר אָנֹכִי מְצַוְּךָ הַיּוֹם לְאַהֲבָה אֶת־יְהוָה אֱלֹהֶיךָ לָלֶכֶת בִּדְרָכָיו וְלִשְׁמֹר מִצְוֹתָיו וְחֻקֹּתָיו וּמִשְׁפָּטָיו וְחָיִיתָ וְרָבִיתָ וּבֵרַכְךָ יְהוָה אֱלֹהֶיךָ בָּאָרֶץ אֲשֶׁר־אַתָּה בָא־שָׁמָּה לְרִשְׁתָּהּ:

Deuteronomy 30:19

הַעִדֹתִי בָכֶם הַיּוֹם אֶת־הַשָּׁמַיִם וְאֶת־הָאָרֶץ הַחַיִּים וְהַמָּוֶת נָתַתִּי לְפָנֶיךָ הַבְּרָכָה וְהַקְּלָלָה וּבָחַרְתָּ בַּחַיִּים לְמַעַן תִּחְיֶה אַתָּה וְזַרְעֶךָ:

because, for; that *(T.I.F.T. Ch 3)*	—	כִּי
mitzvah, commandment *f* *(A.I.E. Ch 2)*	—	מִצְוָה
also appears in plural with pronoun ending: מִצְוֹתָיו		
the *(attached prefix)* *(A.I.E. Ch 1)*, appears on the following words:	—	הַ, הָ

הַמִּצְוָה, הַזֹּאת, הַיּוֹם, הַשָּׁמַיְמָה, הַיָּם, הַדָּבָר, הַחַיִּים, הַטּוֹב,
הַמָּוֶת, הָרַע, הַשָּׁמַיִם, הָאָרֶץ וְהַמָּוֶת, הַבְּרָכָה, וְהַקְּלָלָה

this *f (T.I.F.T. Ch 1)*	—	זֹאת
who, that, which *(A.I.E. Ch 8)*	—	אֲשֶׁר
I *(T.I.F.T. Ch 1)*	—	אָנֹכִי
command, order *(A.I.E. Ch 8), appears in the following words:*	—	צ-ו-ה

מִצְוָה, מְצַוְּךָ, מִצְוֹתָיו

your, you *(attached ending) m sg (A.I.E. Ch 6), appears in the following words:*	—	־ךָ

מְצַוְּךָ, מִמְּךָ, אֵלֶיךָ, בְּפִיךָ, וּבִלְבָבְךָ, לְפָנֶיךָ, אֱלֹהֶיךָ,
וּבֵרַכְךָ, וְזַרְעֶךָ

day *m (A.I.E. Ch 3)*	—	יוֹם
no, not *(B.I.F.B. Ch 3)*	—	לֹא
from, than *(attached preposition) (A.I.E. Ch 10), appears on the following words:*	—	מִ־

מִמְּךָ, מֵעֵבֶר

and *(attached prefix) (A.I.E. Ch 2), appears on the following words:*	—	וְ־, וּ־

וְלֹא, וִיקַחֶהָ, וְיַשְׁמִעֵנוּ, וְנַעֲשֶׂנָּה, וּבִלְבָבְךָ, וְאֵת, וְלִשְׁמֹר,
וְחֻקֹּתָיו, וּמִשְׁפָּטָיו, וְהַמָּוֶת, וְהַקְּלָלָה, וְזַרְעֶךָ

with, in *(attached preposition) (A.I.E. Ch 6), appears on the following words:*	—	בְּ־, בַּ־

בַּשָּׁמַיִם, בְּפִיךָ, וּבִלְבָבְךָ, בִּדְרָכָיו, בָּאָרֶץ, בָּכֶם, בַּחַיִּים

heavens, sky *m (A.I.E. Ch 3)*	—	שָׁמַיִם
saying *(T.I.F.T. Ch 5)*	—	לֵאמֹר
who *(A.I.E. Ch 7)*	—	מִי
go up, ascend *(B.I.F.B. Ch 9), appears in the word* יַעֲלֶה	—	ע-ל-ה
to, for *(attached preposition) (A.I.E. Ch 8), appears on the following words:*	—	לְ־

לָנוּ, לַיָּם, לַעֲשֹׂתוֹ, לְאַהֲבָה, לָלֶכֶת, וְלִשְׁמֹר, לְרִשְׁתָּהּ

toward *(attached ending) (T.I.F.T. Ch 1), appears on the*

following words:	—	זָה
		הַשָּׁמַיְמָה, שָׁמָּה
take *(T.I.F.T. Ch 1)*, appears in the word וַיִּקָּחֶהָ	—	ל־ק־ח
her, it *(attached ending) f sg (A.I.E. Ch 9)*, appears on the *following words:*	—	הָ, יהָ, ־ָהּ
		וַיִּקָּחֶהָ, אֹתָהּ, וְנַעֲשֶׂנָּה, לְרִשְׁתָּהּ
הִפְעִיל: make heard, proclaim *(B.I.F.B. Ch 10)*, appears in the word וַיַּשְׁמִעֵנוּ	—	שׁ־מ־ע
definite direct object marker *(untranslatable) (A.I.E. Ch 4)*, appears seven times	—	אֶת
also appears twice with pronoun ending her: אֹתָהּ		
make, do, act *(A.I.E. Ch 7)*, appears in the *following words:*	—	ע־שׂ־ה
		וְנַעֲשֶׂנָּה, לַעֲשֹׂתוֹ
sea *m (T.I.F.T. Ch 1)*	—	יָם
to, toward *(B.I.F.B. Ch 3)*	—	אֶל
also appears with pronoun ending: אֵלֶיךָ		
word, speech *m (A.I.E. Ch 10)*	—	דָּבָר
heart *m (A.I.E. Ch 6)*, appears in the *word* וּבִלְבָבְךָ	—	לֵבָב
his, him, it *(attached ending) m sg (A.I.E. Ch 9)*, appears on *the following words:*	—	וֹ, ־ָיו
		לַעֲשֹׂתוֹ, בִּדְרָכָיו, מִצְוֹתָיו, וְחֻקֹּתָיו, וּמִשְׁפָּטָיו
see *(T.I.F.T. Ch 3)*, appears in the *word* רְאֵה	—	ר־א־ה
give, grant, permit *(A.I.E. Ch 4)*, appears in the word נָתַתִּי	—	נ־ת־ן
perfect I ending *(T.I.F.T. Ch 4)*, appears on the following *words:* נָתַתִּי, הַעִדֹתִי	—	־תִּי, ־תִי
life *m (A.I.E. Ch 4)*	—	חַיִּים
good *adj (A.I.E. Ch 5)*	—	טוֹב
love *(A.I.E. Ch 6)*, appears in		

the word לְאַהֲבָה	—	א־ה־ב
God m (A.I.E. Ch 4), appears with pronoun ending: אֱלֹהֶיךָ	—	אֱלֹהִים
walk, go (B.I.F.B. Ch 9), appears in the word לָלֶכֶת	—	ה־ל־ך
way, road, path m and f (A.I.E. Ch 9), appears in the word בִּדְרָכָיו	—	דֶּרֶךְ
guard, keep, preserve (A.I.E. Ch 3), appears in the word וְלִשְׁמֹר	—	שׁ־מ־ר
justice, judgment, law m (T.I.F.T. Ch 5), appears in the word וּמִשְׁפָּטָיו	—	מִשְׁפָּט
live, be alive (A.I.E. Ch 8), appears in the following words: וְחָיִיתָ, תִּחְיֶה	—	ח־י־ה
perfect you ending (T.I.F.T. Ch 6), appears on the following words:	—	־תָ, ־תָּ
וְחָיִיתָ, וְרָבִיתָ, וּבָחַרְתָּ		
bless (A.I.E. Ch 1), appears in the following words: וּבֵרַכְךָ, הַבְּרָכָה	—	ב־ר־ך
earth, land f (A.I.E. Ch 3)	—	אֶרֶץ
you m sg (A.I.E. Ch 1)	—	אַתָּה
come (T.I.F.T. Ch 3), appears in the word בָא	—	ב־ו־א
there (B.I.F.B. Ch 5), appears with ending meaning toward: שָׁמָּה	—	שָׁם
your, you (attached ending) m pl (A.I.E. Ch 6), appears in the word בָּכֶם	—	־כֶם
choose, select (A.I.E. Ch 4), appears in the word וּבָחַרְתָּ	—	ב־ח־ר
in order to, so that, for the sake of (T.I.F.T. Ch 7)	—	לְמַעַן
imperfect you prefix (T.I.F.T. Ch 6), appears on the word תִּחְיֶה	—	־תִּ
seed, offspring m (B.I.F.B. Ch 7), appears in the word וְזַרְעֶךָ	—	זֶרַע

Translating the Torah Study Text [pages 115–117]

As your students work on their translations, the following comments may assist them:

1. The definite article הַ is often included in Hebrew on nouns indicating abstract concepts, such as "peace," "love," and so forth. An example of this appears in verse 15 with the words אֶת־הַחַיִּים וְאֶת־הַטּוֹב וְאֶת־הַמָּוֶת וְאֶת־הָרָע, "the life and the good and the death and the evil," and in verse 19 with the words הַחַיִּים וְהַמָּוֶת, "the life and the death and the words הַבְּרָכָה וְהַקְּלָלָה, "the blessing and the curse." In English, the definite article "the" sounds awkward in these instances and is omitted in three of our four translations.

2. As noted several times previously, prepositions can have a range of meanings depending on the context. In verse 19, the preposition בְּ is rendered in all four of our translations as "against," in the phrase הַעִדֹתִי בָכֶם הַיּוֹם, "I call as witness **against** you today."

3. It has also been noted previously that the reversing *vav* can have a range of different meanings—"and/then/so/now"—as well as being left untranslated (except for reversing the verb). In verse 19, all four of our translations render this reversing *vav* differently:

    JPS: "Choose life"

    ArtScroll *Chumash*: "and you shall choose life"

    Everett Fox: "now choose life"

    Jerusalem Bible: "therefore, choose life"

[pages 117–119]

The JPS translation is the only one that does not give a literal translation of the words

אֶת־הַחַיִּים וְאֶת־הַטּוֹב וְאֶת־הַמָּוֶת וְאֶת־הָרָע, "the life and the good and the death and the evil," in verse 15. While there are slight variations among the other three translations, such as whether or not to include the definite article "the" (which only the ArtScroll *Chumash* includes) or whether to translate רַע as "evil" or as "ill," the other three translations essentially provide the literal meaning of the Hebrew words. The JPS translation is different: "life and prosperity, death and adversity," which is an interpretation of the meaning of the Hebrew words.

Vocabulary [page 119]

All the new vocabulary words are identified and highlighted within the Torah Study Text at the beginning of Chapter 10, on page 126.

The word לִפְנֵי, "before," appears with the ךָ, "you," pronoun ending: לְפָנֶיךָ, "before you."

The words מָוֶת, "death," and רַע, "evil," only appear with the definite article ה.

The Hebrew Root [pages 120–121]

The forms of the root ע־ב־ר contain the slight variations in vowels characteristic of verbs with the first root letter ע, such as ע־ב־ד and ע־מ־ד. The word יַעֲבֹר in verse 13 is an imperfect הוּא form. The word עֵבֶר, appearing twice in verse 13, is a noun meaning "region across" or "beyond/side," but it is used like a preposition in the combinations מֵעֵבֶר לְ, "from across/beyond," and אֶל עֵבֶר, "to across/beyond."

The root מ־ו־ת, like the root ב־ו־א, is characterized by its middle root letter ו, which drops out in many verb forms.

Exercises

Exercise 2 [page 123]

2. Draw a line connecting each Hebrew word to its English translation. For some words, there can be more than one correct translation.

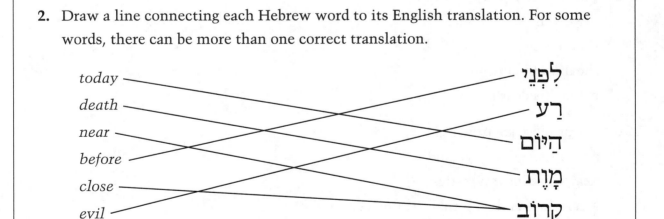

today   לִפְנֵי
death   רַע
near   הַיּוֹם
before   מָוֶת
close   קָרוֹב
evil

Exercise 3 [page 123]

3. The following are plural forms of words introduced as vocabulary in this chapter. Draw a line connecting each plural word to its singular form. Translate both into English.

evil (f pl) _____	רָעוֹת	קָרוֹב	close, near (m sg) _____
close, near (m pl) _____	קְרוֹבִים	קְרוֹבָה	close, near (f sg) _____
close, near (f pl) _____	קְרוֹבוֹת	רַע	evil (m sg) _____
evil (m pl) _____	רָעִים	רָעָה	evil (f sg) _____

Exercise 4 [page 123–124]

a. before Moses

   before me

   before you *(m sg)*

   before him

   before you *(m pl)*

b. the path/road/way of death

   my death

   their death

   the day of her death

   before his death

c. a near/close [nearby] light

   a near/close [nearby] land

   near/close [nearby] cities

   Near/close is the Eternal to all/every [one]

   Close to us is the man. {The man is close to us. *or* The man is a relative of ours.}

d. the eye of evil (the evil eye)

   an evil heart

   an evil act/deed

   an evil spirit

   an evil face *or* evil faces

e. until today

before today

after today

like/as today

behold/here is the day *or* behold/here today

Exercise 5 [pages 124–125]

Translation	Form		Root	Verb
die *(m pl)*	פָּעַל	participle	מ־ו־ת	מֵתִים
pass, cross *(m sg)*	פָּעַל	participle	ע־ב־ר	עוֹבֵר
pass, cross *(f pl)*	פָּעַל	participle	ע־ב־ר	עוֹבְרוֹת
cause to pass, bring across *(m sg)*	הִפְעִיל	participle	ע־ב־ר	מַעֲבִיר
cause to die, kill *(m sg)*	הִפְעִיל	participle	מ־ו־ת	מֵמִית
I will/shall/may *or* let me die	פָּעַל	imperfect	מ־ו־ת	אָמוּת
you *(m pl)* will/shall/may die	פָּעַל	imperfect	מ־ו־ת	תְּמוּתוּ
you *(m pl)* will/shall/may pass/cross	פָּעַל	imperfect	ע־ב־ר	תַּעֲבְרוּ
you *(m pl)* will/shall/may bring across	הִפְעִיל	imperfect	ע־ב־ר	תַּעֲבִירוּ
I will/shall/may *or* let me cross/pass	פָּעַל	imperfect	ע־ב־ר	אֶעֱבֹר
I will/shall/may/let me bring across	הִפְעִיל	imperfect	ע־ב־ר	אַעֲבִיר
I brought across/caused to pass	הִפְעִיל	perfect	ע־ב־ר	הֶעֱבַרְתִּי
you *(m sg)* crossed/passed	פָּעַל	perfect	ע־ב־ר	עָבַרְתָּ
he caused to die/killed	הִפְעִיל	perfect	מ־ו־ת	הֵמִית
they caused to die/killed	הִפְעִיל	perfect	מ־ו־ת	הֵמִיתוּ

Notes on

Chapter 10 · Unit Five

Torah Study Text: Vocabulary and Root Review [page 126]

Vocabulary words that appear in our Torah Study Text in variant forms or with prefixes or suffixes attached were noted in the Vocabulary section of the previous chapter of this Teacher's Guide. The various forms of the new roots מ־ו־ת and ע־ב־ר were explained in the Hebrew Root section of the previous chapter of this Teacher's Guide.

Building Blocks

Perfect Forms [page 127]

You may wish to point out to your students that the word קִדְּשָׁנוּ, "has sanctified us," (the הוּא perfect verb קִדֵּשׁ with the נוּ, "us," pronoun ending attached), is the verb form that appears in blessings for the performance of a mitzvah: אֲשֶׁר קִדְּשָׁנוּ בְּמִצְוֹתָיו. This is NOT an example of an אָנוּ or אֲנַחְנוּ perfect verb form.

The regular פָּעַל perfect אֲנַחְנוּ or אָנוּ form is ■ָ■ַ■ְנוּ.

The regular פִּעֵל perfect form is ■ִ■ַּ■ְנוּ.

The regular הִפְעִיל perfect form is: הִ■ְ■ַ■ְנוּ. The example הֶעֱבַרְנוּ, "we transported/brought across," contains a slight variation in the vowels caused by the first root letter ע.

Imperfect Forms [page 127]

There are many variations in the vowels of imperfect forms, caused by various root letters.

The regular פָּעַל imperfect form is נִ■ְ■ֹ■, but most of the verb roots introduced do not follow this regular pattern, but contain some variation in vowels due to root letters ע, ח, ה, א, or י or ו. The example נֹאמַר, "we will say/let us say," contains a variation in the vowels caused by the first root letter א.

The regular פִּעֵל imperfect form is נְ■ַ■ֵּ■.

The regular הִפְעִיל imperfect form is: נַ■ְ■ִי■.

You may wish to mention to your students that when אָנוּ or אֲנַחְנוּ imperfect verb forms appear in the prayer book, they are generally translated as "let us." The word נֹאמַר appears, for example, at the end of the מִי שֶׁבֵּרַךְ, the prayer for healing, in the phrase: וְנֹאמַר אָמֵן, "and let us say amen."

Additional Reading and Translation Practice [pages 131–134]

1. גְבוּרוֹת can be found in the gender-sensitive *Gates of Prayer* on page 57.

2. The קְדוּשָׁה can be found in the gender-sensitive *Gates of Prayer* on page 116.

3. עֲבָדִים הָיִינוּ can be found in *The Open Door Haggadah* on page 32.

4. Psalm 137:1 can be found in *Shireinu Songbook: A Songbook for Camps, Conclaves, Kallot and Retreats* (2nd edition) on page 2.

5. The opening statement for בִּרְכַּת הַמָּזוֹן can be found in *On the Doorposts of Your House* on pages 9–10.

Exercises

Exercise 1 [page 135]

Translation	Form	Root	Verb
we will/shall/may *or* let us go up/ascend	imperfect	ע־ל־ה	נַעֲלֶה
we will/shall/may *or* let us choose	imperfect	ב־ח־ר	נִבְחַר
we passed/crossed	perfect	ע־ז־ר	עָזַרְנוּ
we built	perfect	ב־נ־ה	בָּנִינוּ
we knew	perfect	י־ד־ע	יָדַעְנוּ
we will/shall/may *or* let us walk/go	imperfect	ה־ל־ך	נֵלֵךְ
we will/shall/may *or* let us speak	imperfect	ד־ב־ר	נְדַבֵּר
we will/shall/may *or* let us praise	imperfect	ה־ל־ל	נְהַלֵּל
we healed	perfect	ר־פ־א	רָפֵאנוּ
we will/shall/may *or* let us stand	imperfect	ע־מ־ד	נַעֲמֹד
we will/shall/may *or* let us take	imperfect	ל־ק־ח	נִקַּח
we will/shall/may *or* let us fear/be in awe	imperfect	י־ר־א	נִירָא
הִפְעִיל: we were kept alive	perfect	ח־י־ה	הֶחֱיִינוּ
הִפְעִיל: we will/shall/may *or* let us bring out	imperfect	י־צ־א	נוֹצִיא
הִפְעִיל: we will/shall/may *or* let us kill/put to death	imperfect	מ־ו־ת	נָמוּת

2. In each of the following phrases or sentences, circle the one form in the parentheses that is grammatically correct. Translate.

a. יֵשׁ לָנוּ בַּת (אַחַת, רַע, הַגְּדוֹלִים).

We have {there is to us} one _____

daughter. _____

b. הָלַכְנוּ אֶל הַמָּקוֹם (קָדוֹשׁ, הַקָּרוֹב, אַחֶרֶת).

We went/walked to _____

the near[by]/close place. _____

c. רָאִינוּ אֶת אַחֵינוּ (חוֹלוֹת, גִּבּוֹר, הַחוֹלִים).

We saw/did see/were _____

seeing/had seen/have seen our sick brothers. _____

d. נָנוּחַ קָרוֹב לַשַּׁעַר (הָאַחֵר, גְּדוֹלָה, קְדוֹשִׁים).

We will/shall/may _____

{Let us/May we} rest near/close to the other gate. _____

e. נְכַבֵּד נָשִׁים (רֵעִים, רַבּוֹת, אֶחָד) בְּתוֹךְ הָעֵדָה.

We will/shall/ _____

may {Let us/May we} honor/respect many women within the community/

congregation. _____

f. אָנוּ נוֹתְנִים נֵר (קְדוֹשָׁה, טוֹבוֹת, גִּבּוֹר) לְרֵעֵינוּ בַּחֹשֶׁךְ.

We give/are giving/do give a mighty light/lamp to our

friends/neighbors/companions/fellows in the darkness.

From Our Texts: "Hava Nagila" [page 138]

The words נָגִילָה, "let us rejoice," נִשְׂמְחָה, "let us be happy," and נְרַנְּנָה, "let us sing with joy," are all אֲנַחְנוּ, "we," forms. Technically, these forms are known as "cohortative" forms, imperfect "we" forms that have the syllable הָ added for emphasis and are usually translated "let us."